She needed him to live!

Upstairs, the nurse at the desk didn't want to let Susannah into Sam's room. She pointed toward the door. "You see that sign? It says DO NOT ENTER. It's for your protection, Miss Grant."

"Oh, for heaven's sake!" Susannah cried. "I've already been exposed in ER, before we knew what anyone had. I am *going* in to see my brother. I'll suit up. I'll even wear goggles. But I *am* going in there."

And she did. The nurse gave in. There *were* advantages to being Samuel Grant's daughter.

Feeling strange in the weird protective gear, Susannah sat beside Sam's bed, holding the hand that hadn't been pierced with an IV needle, talking to him in a low, steady voice. He lay perfectly still, his face ashen, his eyes closed, the monitor at his head reflecting a steady zigzagging line that reassured Susannah. As long as that line wasn't flat . . .

MED CENTER

Virus
Flood
Fire

MED CENTER

DIANE HOH

virus

SCHOLASTIC INC.
New York Toronto London Auckland Sydney

No part of this publication may be reproduced in whole or in part, or stored in a retrieval system, or transmitted in any form or by any means, electronic, mechanical, photocopying, recording, or otherwise, without written permission of the publisher. For information regarding permission, write to Scholastic Inc., 555 Broadway, New York, NY 10012.

ISBN 0-590-54322-9

12 11 10 9 8 7 6 5 4 3 2 1   6 7 8 9/9 0 1/0

Printed in the U.S.A.   01

First Scholastic printing, July 1996

MED CENTER

virus

chapter

1

Hot. So hot. Every inch of her being roasted over hot coals. Her skin, when she touched it tentatively, felt as dry as dust, and her eyes burned as if she were staring directly into the sun.

She didn't understand it. Like most of the other day-camp counselors in the lush, heavily treed playground at Grant Med Center, she was wearing white shorts, a red tank top, and sneakers. The temperature hadn't yet gone above eighty, and there was a cool breeze that ruffled her long, sleek blonde hair and set the only unoccupied swing gently swaying.

The breeze should have cooled her body, but it hadn't. Not a cool spot from her toes to the top of her head. Not a drop of saliva remained in her mouth. It felt full of wool. If she had been required to speak, she was certain no sound would have made it through that arid thickness.

She couldn't be sick again so soon. She had thought she was completely over that rotten bout with the flu. It couldn't come back now. Boring old school was finally over, and summer was here. Why couldn't this have happened while classes were still in session? Maybe she'd have missed that last fatal geometry test and been spared her mother's endless lecture about the importance of a good education. If the flu was going to hit her again, why hadn't it done so then? Until a few days ago, she'd felt fine. Or was it a week ago? She wasn't sure. How could she think with her brain on fire?

A spasm of coughing seized her as she moved slowly, wavering slightly, to catch the toddlers whizzing down the sliding board. The spasm caught her off guard. She'd had others, the night before and again this morning, but this one was the worst by far. In seconds, she was doubled in half, as if someone had delivered a blow to her stomach. Her hands went to her mouth. Her knees bent under the strain of one hoarse, body-wrenching cough after another.

The children at the very top of the sliding board, awaiting their turns, stared, wondering what was happening. She wasn't their favorite counselor, always whining about something or other, but she was okay. So they waited for someone to come to her aid.

The boy who did was tall, dark-skinned, handsome. Fortunately for the girl, Will Jackson was a paramedic, not yet on duty at Med Center's Emergency Services. He knew the signs of serious physical distress when he saw them. He had come to the playground to deliver his six-year-old nephew, but stopped en route to the oversized, crowded sandbox when he saw what was happening. Calling out the girl's name, he rushed over to her, at the same time waving commandingly to two other counselors standing near the monkey bars to join him.

The three ran together to the girl's aid.

By that time, her knees had given way completely. She sank to the ground, still wracked with the agonizing coughing. Her hands went to her chest in a desperate effort to remove the iron bands squeezing the breath out of her. A moment later, her eyes rolled back in her head and, face scarlet, she toppled sideways, landing gently in the soft, sand-filled pit at the foot of the sliding board.

The coughing stopped. She let out a little sigh of relief and closed her eyes, her fevered body going completely limp.

When Will Jackson reached her, the other two counselors right behind him, a vivid scarlet rash had sprung to life on the girl's chest, clashing with the red of her tank top.

"Call Emergency!" Will barked, waving a hand toward the tallest of the cluster of brick buildings encircling the playground. "Get an ambulance!" He crouched beside the stricken girl. "Something is really wrong here."

He was right.

Something was very wrong.

In the far south end of Grant, in a small building that could only be called a shack, precariously perched on a slope above the riverbank, a young man in T-shirt and jeans prepared to leave for his summer job as a window washer. His efforts at leaving some sort of order behind him were desultory. Even on good days, he tended to leave his coffee cup sitting on the table, the brown liquid coagulating into a sticky residue by late afternoon when he returned. He never made up his narrow cot in the tiny back room of the shack, figuring he was just going to mess it up again that night, anyway, and he washed dishes no more than once a week, usually at that point when he could no longer find a clean glass or coffee mug or spoon. That was on good days.

But today was not a good day. On this particular Monday morning, Jenkins Rue was feeling like a tennis ball at the end of a long match between champions. He knew it was his own fault. He'd stayed out late both Saturday and Sunday nights, dancing his boots off at The Music Room, a club downtown. Couldn't tear himself away, and now he was regretting it.

It was way too hot for so early in the morning. What had happened to the usual cool breeze from the river? Bad enough he had to live in this hellhole. Was a little breeze too much to ask for?

If he didn't show up at work, he wouldn't get paid. He needed that money. The only way he was ever going to have a chance with someone like Tina Montgomery was with a college degree hanging on one of his walls, and that took big bucks. It wasn't as if he had parents to hand him a tuition check, like Tina did. Hell, her parents could *buy* her a college if they wanted to. His, on the other hand, had crashed their Harley into a tree ten months ago. They hadn't been wearing helmets ("Not cool" his mother had said) and they weren't the type to buy insurance. If his grandfather hadn't left him this old fishing shack, Jenkins Rue would be living on the streets.

Man, this headache! Felt like his brain had swollen to three times its normal size. Weird, too, because Tina had complained about having a bad headache last night. He'd thought she was just trying to get rid of him. Maybe not. Were headaches catching? His throat hurt, too, and he couldn't stop hacking away like a heavy smoker, which he wasn't. Tina had been coughing, too.

Damn. He couldn't afford to get sick.

Maybe once he got outside, the fresh air would take care of it. If it didn't, he'd down a couple of aspirin and go to work, anyway.

Without combing his thick mass of shoulder-length, light brown, curly hair, Jenkins Rue left the riverbank shack for his window-washing job.

He made it to work at the University Health Club without slamming into a tree or another vehicle.

His window-washing routine never varied. The health club on Mondays. The rest of the week he spent at Med Center, doing whichever of the eighteen buildings he was assigned to. Jenkins wished he were doing the lab today. Although it was huge and took forever to do, it was only two stories high. With his stomach so queasy and his head splitting, he wasn't keen on taking the scaffolding up to the top of the eighth-floor fitness center. But this was Monday.

Coughing hard, Jenkins wiped a brow that burned beneath his hand, and stepped onto the mechanized scaffolding, grasping the side railing with both hands after he had pushed the button to send himself skyward.

He was between the second and third floors, directly above a wide cement driveway, when a wave of dizziness assailed him and he staggered sideways a step or two. If he hadn't been coughing so hard, he would have righted himself easily and regained his footing.

That didn't happen. The spasm was much worse than the preceding ones. It watered his eyes and made breathing difficult. Dizzy and disoriented, Jenkins made a fatal mistake. Instead of taking a step or two back to the right, he mistakenly attempted to step to his left, sending his left foot completely off the platform into empty space and tilting Jenkins off balance.

Two and a half floors above the driveway, he flew out into the air, seemed to hang there for a fraction of a second, and then plunged straight down, arms and legs flailing.

A red-and-white ambulance, with the words GRANT MEDICAL CENTER printed on its sides in huge, black, block lettering, sped away from Emergency Services and raced through town, turning left at the end of the driveway, toward the day-care center.

Its siren screamed throughout the early morning quiet of the city of Grant, Massachusetts, without pause until it reached its destination. Then it died abruptly.

chapter
2

Susannah Grant had been trying for ten minutes to get the attention of her father, Samuel Grant II, a tall, distinguished-looking man with thick white hair and keen blue eyes, wearing an impeccably tailored gray suit over a two-hundred-dollar white shirt and a red silk tie. He sat in his customary place at the head of the long, oval, antique table in the dining room of Linden Hall, the family's elegant stone and white-frame mansion. He wasn't responding to his daughter because he was deeply engaged in conversation with his son, Samuel Grant III, sitting on his father's right.

Susannah, sitting opposite her twin, glared at both of them. Basketball scores! Heads bent, leaning earnestly toward each other, they were talking about the past weekend's athletic events as if the discussion might bring about an end to world hunger. They seemed totally unaware of Susannah or her mother, Caroline, who poked listlessly at her fruit cup at the opposite end of the table.

Susannah turned in exasperation to her mother. "Why do I always feel, when I'm sitting at this table, that I've suddenly become invisible?"

Caroline glanced up, her beautiful face a blank. Deep blue eyes, the same exact shade as her children's, were distant, as if she'd just awakened from a dream. "Did you say something, dear?"

Susannah sighed in defeat and reached up to brush a thick wave of blonde hair away from her forehead. Her irritated gaze returned to father and son. "I wouldn't want to interrupt the most important sports discussion held in the state of Massachusetts in this century, but I need to ask Dad something."

Caroline nodded vaguely and said, "Yes, of course. Go right ahead, dear." She returned to her grapefruit and orange wedges.

Susannah sighed. No help there. Temporarily giving up, she sat back in her chair, glancing around the dining room as she waited for a lull in the conversation that excluded her. It was a pretty room with cobalt blue walls and shiny marble floors. An imported crystal chandelier was centered over the table, which easily seated twenty people. Baskets and vases of brightly colored summer flowers, courtesy of the efforts of Paolo, the gardener, were perched on the sideboard and on a long, low table behind Sam. The early morning sun, streaming in through a wall of French doors leading to a stone terrace, striped the gleaming hardwood floor.

Susannah's eyes moved to survey the people in the room. Sam was so good-looking, Susannah decided, watching him, that he could easily have been in the 100 Most Beautiful People issue of one of those popular celebrity magazines. A recent cover had featured a young man — hadn't it been one of the Kennedys? — who wasn't any better-looking than Sam. The only difference was, that guy had had dark hair and eyes, while Sam's hair was sun-streaked blonde, like hers, and although they were not identical twins, he, like she, had their mother's brilliant blue eyes. Minus the faint look of sadness.

Nothing sad about Sam. Life of the party. And why not? If anyone in Grant, Massachusetts, had the world by the tail, the heir to the Grant fortune certainly did. Girls, parties, fun, money. The story of Sam's life.

If we were identical, Susannah thought not for the first time, I'd be gorgeous, too. And I'd be tons of fun, like Sam. Not only do we not look that much alike except for coloring, but our personalities are as different as Mother's and Dad's.

Caroline Grant sat at the far end of the table, as if, Susannah thought, she'd been banished there for breaking a house rule. Something Caroline would never, ever do. Even at seven-thirty in the morning, every auburn hair was in place, makeup perfectly applied, and she was fully dressed in pale blue silk, looking every inch the wealthy, well-bred wife of the most powerful man in town.

So why didn't she look ecstatically happy?

Although Susannah's mother seemed remote at times, she always functioned perfectly as the head of their busy household. She kept herself fit and trim, entertained beautifully, and was popular with the other wives of Grant "society." If she found a spare moment, she quite often spent it trying to persuade her only daughter to cultivate more friends. Susannah interpreted that to mean "Try to be more like Sam" and ignored the advice. She loved her brother, but his hectic life of fun and games wasn't for her. She loved dancing, but she also liked quiet times with friends, and walks along the riverbank that bisected the city of Grant. Secretly, she believed her mother would have preferred a quieter lifestyle, too. But there were parties to go to, charitable affairs to organize and attend, entertaining to do. If her mother had wanted to stop and smell the roses, she'd married the wrong man. She should have married Paolo, the gardener, instead.

Through the sparkling glass of the French doors, Susannah could see, far below, the mass of eighteen red brick buildings, some ivy-covered, some tall, some shorter and wider, that made up the world-famous medical complex known as Med Center, where she did volunteer work in Grant Memorial's Emergency Services. Surrounded by the city of Grant, the vast, sprawling complex was almost a city in itself. She yearned to be down there, where she was the happiest.

Suddenly impatient to get going, Susannah said quickly, "Dad, can I take the Jeep today?"

Without lifting her head, Caroline corrected automatically. "May I, dear, not can I."

The forkful of omelet halfway to Samuel Grant's mouth paused in midair. He frowned at his daughter, as if he'd forgotten she was sitting there and was startled to hear the sound of her voice. But it was only her request that caused the frown. "The Jeep? I bought that for Paolo, Susannah. It's strictly for running errands, hauling supplies, and off-road driving to check the property." He smiled tolerantly at her. "It probably smells of fertilizer. What's wrong with your own car?"

He had given her, for her sixteenth birthday, a sleek, silver Benz convertible. Susannah hated it. Only two people fit in that car. If she wanted to include a third person — Kate Thompson, for instance, or Will Jackson — where would she put them? Neither was small enough or contortionist enough to cram into the tiny space behind the leather bucket seats.

Not that she spent that much social time with either Will or Kate. But that didn't mean she didn't want to.

Her father never would have bought Sam such a small car. Instead, Sam had a top-of-the-line van, also silver, loaded with the latest automotive features. In it, he hauled the basketball team from his private day school, the soccer team, the squash and jai alai teams. If it was a sport, Sam played it. And if he played it, he excelled at it.

His twin excelled at no sport. She played softball and basketball well, and was a fairly good dancer. But she didn't excel. "Nothing's wrong with my car. Except what I've said all along. It's too small, Dad."

Samuel Grant laughed, showing perfect white teeth, startling in a face so deeply tanned. Although as head of Grant Pharmaceuticals he was a very busy man, he found time for enough golfing, swimming, and tennis to maintain the physique of a man half his age. "Well, I could have given you a Caddy, Susannah. But what would you want with a car that size?"

She knew perfectly well what he meant. He meant that she wasn't the Cadillac type. *He* was. He fit into big, expensive cars. So did her mother. And Sam would, when he was older. But not her.

"I'd rather have the Jeep," she forged on stubbornly. "I already checked with Paolo. He doesn't need it today."

When her father had given in, Susannah excused herself, a needless gesture since no one paid any attention to her departure, and left the house.

Her disgruntled attitude left her, as it always did, when she was outside. Tall and slender, her long, wavy, pale hair caught up in a neat French braid, Susannah stood with her hands on jeaned hips, looking down at the city below. Her eyes lit up as they always did when they focused on Med Center, the sprawling medical complex.

She couldn't wait to get down there. There was life in the dozen and a half buildings set on velvety, rolling green lawns among huge old maple and oak trees. *Real* life. There was, of course, death, too, and heartache and tragedy. But she preferred to think of the center as a place of life and hope. She called the complex MC for short, which she wrote as "Emsee" when she sent letters to her maternal grandparents in Florida.

The Grant family had made their fortune in railroads. Since World War II, they had made a new fortune in pharmaceuticals and surgical instruments. The family, over the one hundred years since the hospital had been founded, had been the main financial contributor to Med Center.

To Susannah, Emsee was the very heart of

Grant, Massachusetts. Without the complex and its companion, Grant University, no blood would flow through Grant's veins, no oxygen would reach its lungs or brain, and it would wither and die.

Grant Memorial, the tallest building in the complex, was where she did most of her volunteering, in the ER. She was happier in that building than anywhere else on earth. And proud. She was proud to be a part of it. Wherever she was in town, whatever she was doing, when she heard a siren split the air, she knew the staff at Emergency would hear the sound, too, and all would be on the alert. Traffic accidents, heart attacks, floods, fires, explosions, whatever, the best medical staff in the world would do everything in their power to keep the incoming patient or patients alive. Even when the injuries were minor, requiring only medication, sutures, or a bandage and reassurance, Susannah was glad to be a small part of the process.

She climbed into the Jeep, feeling the sun on her face. It was the pace of Emsee that she loved the most. Day after day, the admissions at Emergency came in fast and furiously, handled with what Susannah thought of as "controlled chaos." When the EMTS arrived with an ambulance, they barked out vital statistics at a breathless pace, and nurses and orderlies rushed with the gurney into a treatment room. What followed was a mad, noisy, adrenaline-fueled race to save a life before the "Golden Hour," the period that could make all the difference between life and death for a critically ill or injured patient, could expire. And yet there was a purposeful design to those frenetic, tension-filled moments, a concerted effort to put together the pieces to the medical puzzle in time to save a life.

They were busy in ER even when the emergencies were mostly minor. On any given day, ER could have as many as ten people in the waiting room, five or six, even seven in various treatment rooms, and more patients lying on gurneys or in chairs awaiting X rays, exams, or stitches for minor cuts.

"Never a dull moment," Will, a busy paramedic, often said as he ran past Susannah alongside one of the wheeled stretchers.

He was right. If Emsee was the heart of Grant, Massachusetts, then Grant Memorial's ER was the heart of Emsee, and that was where Susannah wanted to be.

She put the Jeep in gear and drove, faster than she should have, down the steep, winding hill to Med Center.

At the University Health Club, an ambulance screeched to a halt, and Will Jackson and two other paramedics jumped clear.

16

Jenkins Rue was conscious and able to tell them that he had fallen.

Will glanced up at the building. Jenkins had fallen almost three stories. How could he still be conscious?

He had no neck pain, he said, but his left elbow jutted out oddly. Dislocation, Will told himself, kneeling beside the victim. And his left femur was clearly fractured. Not a clean break, either. Jenkins was going to need surgery and he could probably kiss his football career good-bye.

Will began reading off statistics. "Pulse 92, respiration 18, blood pressure 118/70." He would not normally have taken the patient's temperature at that point until they had the cervical collar on and light traction applied to the leg. But when his hand came in contact with Jenkins's skin, he knew immediately that the heat of it wasn't only from the hot sun. "He's hot, man," he said to his partners, "burning up."

When they had done the best they could with the injured leg by dressing the open wound and applying gentle traction, they immobilized the possibly dislocated elbow with a well-padded pair of ladder splints and carefully, gently, transferred the patient to an aluminum scoop stretcher before putting him on the gurney.

"When you call in," Will told his partner as they climbed aboard the ambulance, "mention the temp, okay? It's 102. They'll need to know that." He wasn't nearly as concerned about Jenkins's injuries as he was about the high fever. The leg was going to need surgery, and the high temperature complicated things.

Contact with the hospital by radio brought orders for an IV of normal saline for Jenkins and the application of antishock trousers. Because of the leg injury, the trousers were to be applied only to the uninjured leg and the abdomen. It would have to be done carefully.

When that had been done, Will's partner completed the cursory physical exam. No evidence of chest injury, yet the lungs didn't sound clear, as they should have.

"I think he's probably got the flu," Will said.

Hospital staff members were standing by when they arrived at Med Center. A nurse took a new set of vital signs as they hurried along the corridor with the gurney, and Will quickly pointed out the unusually high temperature. The temp was important. Because Jenkins wasn't in any danger of bleeding to death and the initial examination in the ambulance hadn't detected any sign of internal injuries, the fractured leg in itself wouldn't be given high priority. But the temp would.

The nurse thanked him and urged the orderly helping her to "Hurry it up!"

Will watched as the stretcher raced down the hallway toward a trauma room, and wondered what the chances were that Tina Montgomery and Jenkins Rue were suffering from the same illness.

chapter
3

On the east side of the city of Grant, in a neighborhood known as Eastridge, where the homes
were small enough to fit into the Grant mansion's sunroom, Kate Thompson raced around
the sunny, clean but disordered kitchen on Per-
simmon Drive, getting ready for her shift at Med
Center, where she, like Susannah, worked as a
volunteer in Emergency Services.

Strong, athletic legs ran from counter to table
to kitchen drawer and back again, carrying an
empty coffee cup and toast-crumbed plate to the
sink, tossing her paper napkin into the yellow
wastebasket, straightening the blue-flowered
plastic tablecloth and wiping it free of crumbs.
In front of the small mirror just inside the
kitchen door, a purple pick raked its way
through a fringe of bangs over dark, long-lashed
eyes. There was a minor adjustment to thick,
black, cornrowed hair. A dab of plum lip gloss
followed, a flick of blusher to high, sharply angled cheekbones, then a pair of heavy wooden
earrings of Kate's own design were hurriedly

thrust into her earlobes, and she was done. Jeans and a white T-shirt were acceptable work gear at Emergency. Sneakers instead of sandals on her feet. Safer footing on the slippery white tiles.

Kate was one of the few volunteers actually allowed into the treatment rooms at ER where the cases in need of instant, expert care were brought. She and Susannah Grant. They had been carefully selected by the Director of Emergency Services because of their grades at school, their interest in medicine, and because, after being interviewed by two psychiatrists at Llewelyn T. Grant Psychiatric Hospital at Med Center, the Director had been assured they could handle whatever came their way.

Kate hadn't been the least bit surprised by the results of her own evaluation. She'd never had much doubt that she could handle the more gruesome aspects of trauma work. But she'd been knocked out when she heard that Susannah Grant, of all people, would be working alongside her. *The* Susannah Grant? *Princess* Grant? For that was how Kate had thought of her, until she got to know her. Blonde and blue-eyed, of course, as all princesses must be. The Grant girlfriend, who didn't even attend public school with the rest of the masses, looked like she'd faint at the first sight of an artery spurting the red stuff.

But she hadn't. Kate had to admit, however reluctantly, that Susannah had handled every horror that had come into Emergency since they'd become volunteers with cool, calm efficiency. Hardly batted an eye, although sometimes her peachy skin turned a shade or two paler if the damage to a victim was particularly gruesome.

Kate had found, also reluctantly, that she really liked Susannah. The girl might not be a barrel of laughs, but that was basically just shyness, Kate felt. This particular Grant, fancy-schmancy mansion or not, was no snob, even if the house she lived in did actually have a *name*. Whoever heard of naming a *house*? Linden Hall. Sounded like one of the buildings on the University's campus.

And Abby O'Connor, someone Kate had met through Susannah, was okay, too. Not that the three of them were best friends or anything. When they did go to the mall or a movie together, Kate's friends from Eastridge who saw them together had plenty of choice comments to make about "those white-bread girls you've been hangin' around with."

Oh, well. Who said life was supposed to be perfect?

Too bad the staff and other volunteers at MC couldn't see how smart and capable Susannah Grant was. It made them nervous to have Samuel Grant's daughter hanging around the place. Stupid. Susannah's father didn't *run* the complex. That monumental job was the responsibility of Caleb Matthews, parent to the biggest snob in town, one Miss Callie Nose-Up-In-The-Air Matthews. You'd think *she* ran the place.

Scooping her heavy shoulder bag off the back of a kitchen chair, Kate left the kitchen. At least Susannah had three allies at Med Center. There was Kate herself, and Kate's mother, head nurse in Emergency, and Will Jackson, a close friend of Kate's. They'd grown up together. Kate suspected that her parents had always hoped she and Will would become more than friends. Hadn't happened. Will's interests lay elsewhere these days. Kate was around Susannah and Will enough to feel the vibes. Not that they'd ever made a move toward each other. Maybe they never would. Life was tough enough without *that* particular complication.

Kate couldn't very well say, "Oh, go for it," which was pretty much how she felt, when neither had confided in her about their feelings for each other. That was *their* business, not hers.

Waiting at the corner for the bus to Med Center, she wondered what kind of mayhem and misery they'd see on this sunny, warm June Monday. It should repel her, she knew that. But it didn't. Partly because along with the mayhem and misery came miracles. She'd seen them with her own eyes. The heart attack victim who died on the table and was resuscitated, promising with great fervor that he would never, ever smoke a cigarette again. His wife wept in gratitude. The teenager whose arm had been ripped from his body by an auger while he was farming, the limb brought to the hospital in a plastic trash bag filled with ice cubes by his very sharp mother. The arm had been surgically reattached by a brilliant and skillful team of surgeons. Kate had seen that boy later, in Rehab. He'd been moving *both* arms, his eyes shining with relief and pride. He might have to quit the wrestling team, but at least he wasn't going to spend the rest of his life with only one arm. The tiny baby in Neonatal ICU, weighing no more than two and a half pounds and looking decidedly unfinished in his Isolette, his red, wrinkled form hooked up to half a dozen wires and tubes. Everyone at the center, nicknaming him "Peanut," had followed his progress. He'd gone home after two months, weighing slightly over five pounds. He was still a little peanut, but he wasn't blind and had no congenital defects, like some preemies. A lucky peanut.

It was endings like that that kept Kate enthralled with Med Center, and daily strengthened her resolve to have a career in medicine. A surgeon, maybe . . . orthopedic? The reattachment of that boy's arm had truly been a miracle. She would do something like that some day.

"Need a lift?" a voice called, and Kate pulled herself away from the image of herself striding down a white corridor, a stethoscope around her neck. She knew the boy leaning out of the old red truck's passenger window to address her. Damon Lawrence. A friend of Will's all through school until Damon dropped out. He was almost as gorgeous as Will, and she'd had a terrible crush on him when she was ten.

"No, thanks." Kate's voice was cool. She'd never heard of Damon getting into any trouble, but she couldn't forgive him for quitting school and ruining his chances of ever leaving Eastridge. He'd had good grades and was a super athlete. Could have had a scholarship, maybe. Why had he quit?

"Oh, come on, Kate," he pleaded, grinning at her. "I never see you anymore. You're always hiding out there at Bones 'n' Blood." His name for Med Center. Kate hated the nickname. Damon wasn't the only one who spoke that way about the complex, she knew that. There *were* people in Grant who resented the Grant family's wealth and power. Many of them extended that resentment to include Med Center.

"Wait till you need us," she retorted. "You'll change your tune fast enough." Hadn't she seen it happen with her own eyes? Someone who had bad-mouthed MC repeatedly would be brought into the place screaming, maybe bleeding, or doubled over in pain, and by the time they left, they couldn't say enough good things about the staff and the care they'd received.

Damon cocked an eyebrow. "Me? I'm healthy as a horse."

"And just as stupid," Kate said, turning away from him with a careless shrug. "Or you'd still be in school."

The grin disappeared. Muttering something Kate couldn't hear, he jerked away from the window and stomped down hard on the gas. The truck roared away.

What a waste! she thought angrily.

A few minutes later, the big blue-and-white bus arrived at the curb with a puff of smoke to pick up Kate and carry her off to Med Center.

chapter
4

Because Abby was teaching an early aerobics class in the Rehab building at Emsee, Susannah didn't have to pick her up as she usually did. She drove straight to the medical complex.

She never ceased to be awed by the very size of the place when she drove in through the open double gates at the entrance to Emergency's parking garage, a gray stone structure ten stories high. She stood at the back entrance to Emergency, glancing around with pride and the excitement that always overtook her when she left her car and was actually on the grounds of Med Center. The dozen and a half brick buildings of varying sizes were devoted to every area of medical care, including the Walter E. Miller Burn Unit, the Hazel Williams Neonatal Center for Infants and Children, the Psych building, and, to her left, the enormous Oncology building, where new strides in cancer treatment were made every day. There wasn't a physical problem that couldn't be treated at Med Center, and treated with the very best of care. And if there *wasn't* a treatment, it was very possible that the lab at Grant Pharmaceuticals, a long, low building nearly hidden from view in a thick grove of trees behind the complex, would come up with something.

Susannah was just turning to enter the building by its back entrance when she heard an approaching siren. Her heart began to pound as it always did at the sound. Someone whose life was in some way endangered was on his or her way to Med Center. She always wondered, as "incoming" arrived, if they realized, in their shock and pain, that they were coming to the right place. The absolutely right place.

She pushed the double swinging doors open and hurried inside, grabbing a smock off the rack beside the nurses' station as she passed it, signing in hurriedly, and then glancing around for some sign of Kate. She was already busy in one of the treatment rooms, Susannah saw through the glass windows, feeling a pang of envy. Kate was rushing around from table to counter to supply cabinet as a team of hospital personnel worked on a patient. Everyone in Emergency trusted Kate Thompson implicitly. Maybe it was because her mother was ER's head nurse. Whatever the reason, Kate had been asked to help in ten times the number of trauma cases that Susannah had.

Susannah knew that wasn't likely to change.

Not as long as she was Samuel Grant's daughter, and she expected to be that for the rest of her life.

The double doors burst open, and the EMTS raced in pushing a gurney, an IV held high above the patient's head.

Susannah ran ahead of the rushing gurney to fling open the double doors to a treatment room, then stood back and watched as the paramedics ran inside pushing the wheeled cart. Urgent calls went out over the PA system for staff. Susannah remained in the doorway as doctors and nurses came running and the paramedics barked out statistical information about the patient's condition: blood pressure, heart rate, temperature.

Susannah heard "temp, 104," and thought, Oh, wow, there's trouble. 104?

She knew the first moments after a patient arrived at Emergency were the most critical. Every second counted. Sometimes, no matter how prepared the staff was or how efficient, there were not enough moments and they lost the battle. Not often. The entire medical complex had one of the highest patient survival rates in the world, even in Oncology and Cardiac Care. Cancer and heart patients had the best chance of beating their illnesses at Med Center. The ER's survival rate was even higher.

Susannah caught only a glimpse of long, fever-matted blonde hair under the oxygen mask as the gurney raced ahead of her and came to a halt in the middle of the treatment room. The resident on call shouted, "Let's get some fluids into her, stat!"

Stat. Faster than immediately. Susannah nodded. Of course. With a fever that high, they would have to pump fluids into that girl fast.

The young doctor, a resident, took a quick look at the patient and asked the paramedics, "Any history? How long has she been sick? Parents here?"

"She collapsed on a playground. No family around. Will Jackson was going to get in touch with them, but he got called out on a run to the health club. Looks like flu to me, though."

"Get her parents!" the resident ordered. "I need a history."

Then, everyone gathered around the table began calling out statistics and orders at the same time. It was impossible to make out what they were saying, but Susannah knew the gist of it. Fluids in, stat, to combat the patient's dehydration. Dehydration in a human being could be fatal. Take some blood! Type and cross-match! Race the samples to the lab! Pay attention! Do as you're told, no questions asked. Hurry, hurry! No mistakes, this is a *life* in jeopardy here.

A new IV was set up beside the table, then a needle appeared, the first of many. Into the patient's left arm. Taped in place. Then more needles. Some to give aid. Some to take blood. And all the while, poking, prodding, lifting the patient's limbs, testing for mobility, rigidity, examining her eyes, her mouth, her ears, poking, prodding, searching for clues. A nurse repeatedly called to the patient in a loud voice, "Tina? Tina, can you hear me? You collapsed at the playground, Tina, you're at Med Center. Can you tell me where it hurts? How long have you been sick?"

Tina? Susannah knew a Tina. Tina Montgomery. They attended the same private day school. Jenkins Rue had a mad crush on her. But that couldn't be Tina Montgomery on that table. That Tina was strong and healthy. Susannah had seen her the night before, dancing with Jenkins. She hadn't looked sick. Not from a distance, anyway.

Still, that looked like her hair. . . .

More needles, more orders shouted from the attending physician, nurses running from table to supply cabinet, more poking and prodding of the patient. The orders came fast and furiously: aspirin, a refrigerating blanket, alcohol rubs, all designed to bring the dangerously high temperature down.

"Here!" a voice next to Susannah said, as two vials were thrust at her, "get these to the lab, stat!"

Thrilled to help, Susannah whirled and ran. And although she heard another siren die outside the entrance as she ran, she knew there was no time to stop and find out what else was happening. She kept going.

When she returned, another gurney was rushing down the hall toward her. Will Jackson, wearing his navy blue EMT jacket, ran along beside it. She knew better than to ask him any questions as he raced by. But she glimpsed antishock trousers on one of the patient's legs and guessed that the other leg was too seriously injured for confinement. She caught a glimpse of a face that looked as if it had been caved in with a heavy sledgehammer. Drying blood, the soft look of a broken or fractured cheekbone, the puffiness around the eye. If the patient had fallen, he or she must have landed face first.

Trusting the staff to handle this newest emergency, she returned to Tina's treatment room. She stood in the doorway, watching. The work at the table continued just as it had when she left. "Temp, 103," a nurse called out. Down one degree already, Susannah thought with satisfaction. The blanket was working.

When she glanced over her shoulder, the second gurney had disappeared, that patient already in good hands.

Her reaction inside a treatment room during an emergency was always the same. At first glance, it looked like complete and utter chaos. As if no one in the room had the foggiest notion what they were doing. All of the people gathered around the patient shouted at the same time. Two people might be barking out orders for X rays, or a tube down the patient's throat or nose, while someone else called for a chest line or ordered oxygen, or, in extreme cases, a "crash cart" to shock a stilled heart back into action. Still other voices called out vital statistics repeatedly. People scurried around in rubber-soled shoes collecting thermometers or oxygen masks or tubes or IV equipment, while others brought bandages, antiseptic solutions, hypodermic needles, whatever was needed to help the patient.

Although the treatment varied depending upon the state of the patient, the pace was always the same: rushed, frenetic, dizzying, just as it was in this case. Susannah thought of it as miraculous. In the midst of this horrendous, hectic scene, with everyone talking and shouting at the same time, with so many hands reaching across the patient for one piece of medical equipment or another, a life was being saved.

Incredible. That was always her first reaction.

Her second reaction was a fierce yearning to be a more important part of the process than she'd been so far. Was that ever going to happen?

"Miss Montgomery?" A nurse standing at the head of the table called to the patient in a loud voice, "Miss Montgomery, can you hear me?"

Susannah's eyes widened. That really *was* Tina Montgomery on the table.

She remembered then, her mother commenting at dinner one night last week . . . or was it the week before . . . that Tina had the flu. Mrs. Montgomery had told Caroline that Tina was being stubborn about seeing a doctor. Caroline, Susannah remembered now, had been concerned that Tina wouldn't be well enough to model in the Auxiliary's upcoming fashion show. Maybe she wouldn't. This looked a lot worse than a simple case of the flu.

As far as Susannah could tell from where she stood in the doorway, the nurse got no response from the stricken girl.

The tall, heavyset man in white, whom Susannah knew as Dr. Jonah Izbecki, said over the hubbub, "This girl hasn't stopped coughing since they brought her in. Get X Ray down here, stat!"

Because she was standing right beside the wall phone and because she wanted to help, Susannah whirled and picked up the receiver.

And realized she didn't have the faintest idea

how to call X Ray. No one had ever explained the interhospital phone system to her, and no operator came on the line. There were three-digit numbers next to each button, which did her no good at all since she didn't know which number referred to which department.

Kate came through the doorway just then, heard the order for X ray, and immediately sensed Susannah's dilemma. Without taking the receiver, which would have been humiliating for Susannah, Kate quickly reached up and punched in three numbers. Flushing with gratitude, Susannah ordered a portable X-ray unit and hung up, vowing to ask Kate to explain the code to her when (if?) they had a free moment together.

The X-ray order was a little puzzling. What did you X-ray when you suspected a case of the flu? Nothing. But Tina *was* still coughing, a hoarse, wrenching sound that bounced off the white walls. So it had to be Tina's chest that Dr. Izbecki intended to X-ray.

Maybe Tina had pneumonia. That could sometimes be a complication of the flu, especially if the patient ignored the symptoms as Tina had.

If what the patient had was a simple case of pneumonia, it could be treated and conquered with antibiotics. In someone as young and normally healthy as athletic Tina, pneumonia wouldn't be fatal.

But a simple case of pneumonia, Susannah thought with a stirring of uneasiness, wouldn't explain why Dr. Izbecki stepped away from the table just then and said, looking down at Tina, "I don't like this. I don't like this at all. This girl is very sick. She should have seen a doctor long before now. Are her parents here yet?"

His first two sentences seemed strange coming from a man who dealt with accidents and illness on a regular basis. He couldn't like *any* of it, could he? Was it just Tina's delay in seeking medical help that was bothering him? Or was there something else?

An orderly rushed in just then, pushing the portable X-ray machine. Susannah shoved the strange comment out of her mind, concentrating instead on the efforts to care for Tina Montgomery.

Two more doctors arrived, summoned by phone by Dr. Izbecki's nurse. One of them ordered Susannah to "go fetch this girl's parents!"

It wasn't much, but it was something. Susannah turned and ran again.

The first person she saw as she left the treatment room was Will Jackson. Still wearing his navy blue EMT jacket, he was leaning against the buttery-yellow wall in the hallway and sipping a cup of hot coffee. "How is she?" he asked Susannah.

"I don't know. Were you on the run that brought her in?"

"No." He shook his head. His dark eyes regarded Susannah seriously. "But I was at the playground delivering my nephew Benjamin when Tina collapsed. Coughed her lungs out and then just caved. I've never seen anything like it, and that's the truth. When I took her pulse, her skin felt like hot lava was running through her veins. I followed the ambulance in my own car, but the minute I got here, I had to go out on a run. So I hadn't heard how she was doing."

Susannah didn't know Tina Montgomery very well. Tina's father had a really important position at Grant Pharmaceuticals, which Susannah's father owned and ran, and the two families belonged to the same private country club, but Susannah spent little time there. Even if Tina's best friend at school hadn't been Callie Matthews, someone Susannah couldn't stand, she knew that she and Tina never could have been friends. They weren't the same kind of people at all.

Still, Susannah had no wish to see Tina in such dire straits. "I think she had the flu last week or the week before," she said to Will as she began to move on down the hall toward the visitors' waiting room. "Tina's mother told mine. Maybe it came back."

He shook his head negatively again, this time more emphatically. "This isn't the flu. Or if it is, it's a whole new strain, like that swine flu thing a few years back. I've never seen anyone this sick from the flu. Uh-oh," he added, "here come Momma and Poppa Bear."

Susannah turned her head to see a well-dressed couple advancing toward her. The woman was short and too plump for the tennis whites she was wearing, her blonde hair too long and curly for her age. The man was much taller, also slightly overweight, dressed for business in a gray suit. He looked angry, and as they moved up the hallway toward Susannah, she heard him say to the woman at his side, "How could you let it get this bad? The only thing I ask you to do is take care of our daughter, and you can't even do that right? Playing tennis, day and night, is *not* parenting! Meanwhile, my child has fallen so ill that she has to be taken by ambulance to the hospital! And I have to be dragged out of a very important meeting."

Then Astrid Thompson came out from behind her desk and in one smooth, calm movement, stopped the pair from continuing any further, spreading her hands in front of them to act as a barrier. "Mr. and Mrs. Montgomery," she said quietly, "if you'll just wait right here, Dr. Izbecki will be with you shortly. Why don't you have a seat right over there?" She pointed to a cluster of comfortable-looking upholstered chairs and thickly padded blue benches in a wide alcove filled with plants and a table holding a large, silver coffee urn and stacks of white Styrofoam cups.

The VIP suite, Susannah thought dryly.

"Izbecki?" Mr. Montgomery asked. "Listen, I don't want some newcomer with a strange name taking care of my little girl. You get me Joe Landis! Get him down here right now. He's a friend of mine. He'll know what to do for Tina."

"Dr. Landis is a neurologist, Mr. Montgomery," Nurse Thompson answered calmly, taking Mrs. Montgomery's elbow and ushering her gently but firmly into the alcove. "Your daughter doesn't need a neurologist. And Dr. Izbecki has been with us for nearly ten years. I'm surprised you aren't familiar with his name. Your daughter is getting the very best of care. Please don't worry." When she left to summon Dr. Izbecki, Susannah went back to stand beside Will.

She always felt secure when Will was around. He was the youngest paramedic at ER, but he was always so professional, so calm and efficient, reassuring patients in a gentle but firm voice as he ran alongside the gurney to a treatment room. She had come close, many times, to telling him how much she admired his work, but each time she'd hesitated, afraid it would sound patronizing.

She had no way of knowing that praise from her would have made Will Jackson very happy.

"Who was the second incoming? The run you were on?" she asked him quietly. "I heard the ambulance and caught a glimpse of the patient, but I had to run to the lab." She said the last part proudly, glad that she'd been of some use.

"Jenkins," he said grimly.

Susannah gasped. "Jenkins Rue? What happened? He didn't crash on his bike, did he?"

"No. Fell from a scaffolding at the health center. Fell more than two stories. To cement. One leg's a mess, and he could have a head injury."

Susannah's left hand flew to her mouth. "Oh, God, is he . . . is he . . . he's not dead, is he?"

"Wasn't when we brought him in. Pulse thready, though, and I wouldn't want to guess at how many broken bones he's got. But he was still alive. Funny thing, though," Will added, crumpling his cup and tossing it into a nearby wastebasket, "his temp was 103. And that couldn't have been from the fall."

On Susannah's left, the noisy, hectic efforts continued in Tina's treatment room, while behind her, in another hallway, she could hear the same kind of sounds from a different room.

She knew now, her heart sinking at the thought, that what she was hearing was a concentrated effort to keep a friend of hers, a boy named Jenkins Rue, who owned just about nothing, from losing the one thing he *did* own, free and clear. His life.

Telling Will she'd see him later, she turned and raced down the hall to see if she could help. No, not "if." Not this time. This time, she *was* going to help.

chapter
5

Jenkins's room, when she entered, was even more chaotic than Tina's had been. There were at least eight people working on the patient, their hands moving rapidly around his body. Susannah saw blood on the jeans that had been cut away to reveal the injured limb. That was no simple fracture. If he was hoping for an athletic scholarship to college, what would this injury do to his chances?

"Blood pressure falling!" someone at the table shouted. "Eighty over sixty!"

Susannah knew the falling pressure could indicate serious internal injuries. A sharp request for more units of blood quickly followed. A nurse rushed to obey the order. One of the doctors ran to the wall phone to summon an orthopedic surgeon. Susannah recognized the name. The damage must be really bad if Jenkins needed surgery on the leg, instead of a simple setting of the bone, and a plaster cast.

Susannah hesitated just inside the doorway, not sure what to do to make her presence known. When a nurse ran over to the wall to make a call, Susannah said quickly, "If he needs blood, maybe I could give it. Let me do something. I want to *do* something." The nurse nodded, made her phone call, and hung up. But before she returned to the table, she gave Susannah a long look and asked, "You know him?"

"I know who he is. He's not going to die, is he?"

"Don't know yet. Here," she said, handing Susannah a clipboard. "Pay attention to vitals and write them down on here when they're called out. Don't make any mistakes, okay?"

Her stomach churning anxiously, Susannah gripped the board and ran with the nurse back to the table.

Jenkins was unconscious. Tubes and wires ran from his body to various pieces of medical equipment. His skin was chalky, his eyes closed. The entire right side of his face was bloody and beginning to purple, in sharp contrast to the whiteness of his skin. But it was the leg that had suffered the most damage. Susannah had to steel herself to keep from gasping at the sight of the pulpy, bloody mess. Two doctors were working on it at the same time, while two nurses tended to blood pressure and respiration. The very second they called out a new figure, Susannah immediately printed it on the chart in her hands. Her fingers clutched the pen so tightly, her knuckles turned white. She was terrified of making a mistake.

Intent on what she was doing, she jumped, startled, when the orthopedic surgeon who had just arrived barked, "This kid's burning up! I can't operate until he's stable, but the leg won't wait that long."

A hurried, animated discussion between the two doctors began as to the best course of treatment. They continued to work as they argued, and Susannah continued to write down Jenkins Rue's vital statistics as they were called out.

While Susannah worked in Emergency at the rear of the building, a petite, pretty girl wearing a white halter-neck dress and high-heeled white sandals, shiny blonde hair swinging around her shoulders, an unpleasant downturn to her full, pink mouth, hurried with a sense of purpose across the spacious lobby at the front of the building. The pink-smocked woman at the reception desk called out as she passed, "Hello, Miss Matthews. Stopping in to see your father?" She received no response.

Callie Matthews, giving no sign that she had heard the greeting, continued to click-clack in her heels straight to the elevators. She took one of the cages up to the tenth floor. Her father, Caleb Matthews, Med Center's Chief Administrator, and his staff, occupied a suite of offices there that took up all of the tenth and eleventh floors.

Callie loved visiting her father. Nowhere else, not even in their luxurious split-level stone home on the outskirts of Grant, did she feel as strong a sense of power as she did when she stepped out of the elevator onto the thick, copper-colored carpeting. Facing her were dark-paneled walls hung with framed pictures of Grant ancestors and former Med City administrators. Her father's picture would be on that wall one day. In the meantime, the thought that her very own father *ran* this huge, eighteen-building complex known and respected all over the *world* made her feel much taller than her five feet plus one inch.

Of course, she thought as she marched along the hallway toward the door with her father's name on it, there was a downside, too. He was hardly ever home. And her mother was too sick most of the time to be any company. She tried. On her good days, they went shopping and sometimes to the Club, although Althea Matthews, a victim of chronic kidney disease, had long since stopped playing tennis or swimming. Mostly, she just sat, looking even more yellowish and wan than usual in the midst of all the other tanned, healthy mothers.

Callie never would have told anyone, except maybe Tina, but one of the reasons she visited her father so much was, it made her feel better to see how healthy he looked. At least one of her parents wasn't sick. He was losing his hair, and she loathed his choice of ties, always unbelievably garish in color, but he was healthy. Hadn't been sick a day in his life.

So she dropped in as often as she could, even though she knew it sometimes annoyed him because he was so busy. She understood that, because just *think* of all he had to do, running a health complex that last year treated 25,000 patients, performed 14,000 operations, and treated 58,000 patients at Emergency Services. A new patient was admitted every twelve minutes at Med Center, and a new operation begun in the Surgical building or in Emergency every thirty minutes. While she understood how unbelievably busy that made her father's job, she still had a right to see him.

Callie's lips curved upward. Her *father* was the boss of this huge, busy, very important place!

His secretary, Lindsay Cutler, wasn't at her desk outside of his office. Inside taking dictation, maybe. Didn't matter. If she had been there, she wouldn't have tried to keep Callie out unless Caleb was in a very important meeting. Maybe because he knew how hard it was for a teenager to have a semi-invalid mother, her father really did try to make time for her whenever he could. And tall, beautiful Lindsay (incredibly *healthy* Lindsay) had her orders. She was to allow Callie free access to her one healthy parent whenever possible.

Callie grabbed a hairbrush from her white shoulder bag and quickly ran the brush through her hair. Then she marched up to the door that bore her father's name on a polished brass plate near the top and, hoping that he just might take her to dinner at the Club, threw the door open.

To find her father embracing his secretary in the center of the huge, luxurious office.

Callie froze. A sound somewhere between a gasp and a cry left her mouth, startling the pair and causing them to draw apart and turn toward the door. Lindsay had obviously been crying.

"Dad!" Callie accused.

Her father, reading the expression on her face, took a step forward, saying, "Now, wait just a minute, Callie . . ."

Without waiting to hear the rest of what he had to say, Callie whirled and tore out of the room, blonde hair flying out behind her as she ran.

Her father's voice called after her, but she kept going. Instead of heading for the elevators, where she would have to wait and he might catch up with her, she ran to the stairway door and yanked it open. Then she raced down the stairs. When she reached the eighth floor, she left the staircase and emerged into the hall, where she picked up an elevator.

The whole time she was running, Callie had to fight back tears. She would *not* cry, she would *not!* Let that witch Lindsay cry if she wanted to, but not Callie Matthews. Crying was for babies. She wasn't a baby. Hadn't been for a long, long time.

Riding down in the elevator with four student nurses in uniforms, two doctors, and a maintenance man carrying a tool kit, Callie decided angrily that Lindsay had probably only been pretending to cry. Her pathetic attempt at making Caleb Matthews feel sorry for her, just so she could snare him, was disgusting. She'd probably wanted to get her hooks into him ever since the first day she'd come to work at Med Center. She knew he was rich and powerful. And she had to know he had a sick wife. Probably thought that made him an easy target.

And it looked like she'd been right!

At that moment, Callie hated the student nurses, whispering and giggling alongside of her. And she hated the two doctors, with their stupid white jackets and their stupid stethoscopes hanging around their stupid necks. Why did they wear them all the time, anyway? They weren't treating patients in the elevators. Show-offs!

She even hated the maintenance man, because he worked at Med Center. How could she ever have been proud that her father ran this horrible place? If it weren't for Med Center, he'd be home more and he'd have time to take her to dinner once in a while and he wouldn't be hugging Lindsay Cutler. There wouldn't *be* any Lindsay Cutler, at least not in her father's life, if it weren't for Med Center.

She especially hated every single one of the Grants, past, present, and future, because if it weren't for them, there would be no Med Center in the first place. This was all their fault.

If it crossed Callie's mind as she hurried from the elevator that the medical complex she suddenly hated with a fierce rage was also keeping her mother alive, she pushed the thought away. She was too full of shock and fury to think about that now.

As she emerged from the elevator and ran from the building, the pink lady at the reception desk called out cheerfully, "You have a nice day now, Miss Matthews!"

I don't *think* so, Callie thought bitterly as she pushed her way through the glass revolving door.

Tina. She needed Tina. Tina would understand. Tina's father, who worked for Samuel Grant himself at Grant Pharmaceuticals, traveled a lot, so Tina would know better than anyone exactly how Callie was feeling. Maybe that was why they were best friends.

Yeah, right, Callie thought, almost laughing as she emerged, blinking against the bright sunshine. *That's* not why we're best friends. We're best friends because we like the same things.

Nice clothes. Brand-new, expensive sports cars. Tina's canary yellow, mine robin's-egg blue. Even our cars are birds of a feather, so to speak. We like being pretty and well dressed and having money and living in the nicest houses in town and belonging to the country club. What we *don't* like is how hard our fathers have to work to make those things possible.

Tina would definitely understand.

In her robin's-egg blue convertible, Callie drove, very fast, to Tina's house, an enormous red brick colonial nestled in the foothills far below the Grant mansion.

No one answered her ring. Callie frowned in annoyance, as if Tina had deliberately made it a point not to be home when Callie needed her.

Maybe Tina and her mother had gone to the Club. If they had, she'd wangle a dinner invitation with them. Then she wouldn't have to eat alone. Her own mother's dialysis treatment that morning had left her drained. She wouldn't be eating much more than a bowl of soup for dinner, if she ate at all.

And her father was clearly out of the question now as a dinner companion. Probably still comforting Miss Tear-Ducts.

Callie turned around and was about to run down the steps, back to her car, when an elderly man working in his garden across the street called out to her, "You looking for the Montgomery girl?"

She nodded and continued on down the steps.

He walked across the road to meet her at her car. "You haven't heard?"

"Heard what?" Callie pulled her car keys out of her purse.

"Your friend's at the hospital, Miss. My wife heard about it at the Club. Seems your friend collapsed at that day camp over at Med Center. Some kind of flu or something. Her mother came down these steps a little bit ago and tore off in her car. Must have been going to the hospital."

"Hospital?" Callie asked, her mouth suddenly gone dry. "No, that can't be right! Tina can't be in the hospital. She was fine last night. Coughing a little bit, but . . . how sick is she?"

The man shook his head. "Don't know, Miss. The wife and I have been waiting for the girl's parents to get home, so we could ask. Wouldn't want them to think we weren't concerned. But no one's come back yet. Are you one of the girl's friends?"

"I'm her *best* friend," Callie said emphatically. "But I didn't know she was in the hospital."

"You might want to call over there, see how she is, since there's no one here to ask."

"Call? I'm not going to *call!* I'm going over there!" Forgetting to thank him for the information, Callie got back into her car and drove to Med Center, wondering as the car raced along the broad, tree-lined boulevard if anything more could possibly go wrong with this beautiful, sunny, but perfectly horrible June day.

chapter
6

In treatment room number five, where doctors continued to work over Jenkins Rue, Susannah said to a nurse passing by with a syringe, "There's another patient in ER with a high fever."

The nurse stopped in her tracks. "What did you say?"

In spite of the high noise level in the room, the doctors at the table overheard. Heads swiveled to stare at Susannah.

She flushed self-consciously. "I wasn't sure if you knew. They brought in a girl from my school a little while ago. She's really sick. The flu, I guess. Anyway, her temp was 104." She waved a hand toward the table.

"Check it out!" one of the doctors ordered the nurse.

She nodded and handed the syringe to another nurse. "You come with me," she told Susannah. "Show me where the girl is."

They left the room and hurried down the hall to where Susannah had last seen Tina.

The room had been cleared. The table was

bare. A nurse was replacing medical supplies in a wall cabinet. She looked up as Susannah and the nurse opened the door and stood just over the threshold.

Susannah frowned. "What happened to the girl who was in here?"

"Upstairs. ICU."

The Intensive Care Unit. "She's that sick?"

"No diagnosis yet?" the nurse with Susannah asked.

"Flu, maybe. She should have seen a doctor days ago, from the look of things. Dr. Izbecki ordered every culture known to man, and a ton of blood work, but no lab results yet. Too soon. Why?"

"We've got another one, down the hall. Accident victim, but he's burning up with fever. I thought there might be a connection."

"Maybe there is. I know the flu's been going around. We've had quite a few cases in here. None as bad as this girl, though. We got her temp down some, but I wouldn't be surprised if it shot right back up again. Anyway, she's up in ICU. Dr. Izbecki's in the cafeteria having lunch if you need to talk to him."

"Thanks."

As they left the room, the nurse said to Susannah, "I'd better go find Dr. Izbecki. I need more info to take back with me. Why don't you go have lunch? There's nothing more you can do for that boy. You've been a big help. None of us knew there was another patient. Thanks."

Susannah felt a warm glow of satisfaction as the nurse hurried away. She had actually done something to help.

"Hey, Sooz, what's up? Ready for lunch?"

Susannah turned. The only person who ever called her "Sooz" was Abby O'Connor, her best friend. "A *lot* is up," she answered as she faced Abby, who was shorter, darker, and rounder than Susannah, and dressed in khaki pants and a camouflage jacket. "I'll tell you over pasta salad. Have you seen Will? I need to ask him something."

Abby grinned, her dark eyes sparkling. "He's right behind you," she said. "So is Kate." Abby was the only person who knew how much Susannah admired Will Jackson. But she had been sworn to secrecy. She wouldn't tell anyone. Abby wasn't like that. She was loyal to the bone. Susannah would have trusted Abby O'Connor with her life.

When Susannah turned around again, tall, lanky Will was smiling down at her. "What did you want to ask me?"

But before she could ask her question, a door swung open and Callie Matthews burst through it, eyes narrowed, hair flying out around her shoulders. "*Where* is Tina?" she demanded of the quartet gathered near the watercooler. "Someone told me she was here. What's wrong with her? Why didn't somebody tell me?"

"You just said someone *did*," Kate answered coolly. If there was one person who could ruin her day, it was Callie Matthews, tanned a glowing bronze and all dressed up in white like Malibu Barbie.

"I mean, someone from *here*!" Callie snapped. "From Med Center. I had to find out from one of Tina's neighbors that she was sick."

"Well, you're not a relative," Susannah said patiently. "Only relatives are notified when a patient's brought in, Callie." Callie's eyes were slightly pink. Had she been crying because of Tina? Did Callie's feelings go that deep? Hard to believe.

"But I'm her best friend!" Callie glanced up and down the busy corridor. A young man on crutches eyed her appreciatively as he passed, narrowly avoiding crashing into a linen cart. "Where is she, anyway? Can I see her?"

"I don't think so," Will said slowly. "She's up in ICU. No one's allowed in there but family." He pointed toward the alcove. "Her parents are over there, though, if you want to wait with them. They can't go upstairs to see Tina until Dr. Izbecki gives them the go-ahead. Maybe they can give you more information."

Callie hesitated, frowning. "What's wrong with Tina?" Then her pretty, tanned face paled slightly as she added nervously, "It's not catching, is it? What she has?"

Kate let out a scornful half-laugh. "Your concern is so touching, Callie. Don't worry, if it was catching, they'd have put your best friend in Isolation, and they haven't done that. So relax. Anyway, she's probably just got a bad case of the flu."

The boy who came around a corner just then and called out Callie's name was of average height, with wide shoulders and short, blonde hair. He would have been good-looking if a look of discontentment hadn't shadowed his features. He hurried over to the group. "I just heard about Tina," he said as he arrived. "What's the matter with her?"

Jeremy Barlow went to the same private day school that Callie, Tina, and Susannah attended. His father was Emsee's famous, highly respected Chief of Cardiology. Jeremy, whose mother had left her family several years earlier to pursue a writing career in California, spent as much time as possible at Med Center in hopes of catching a few moments with the only parent left to him. Susannah suspected that he and Callie were friends because their family situations were similar. With one major difference: Callie's mother was sick, while Jeremy's had simply walked out of the house one day with two suitcases and a laptop computer. And without her son.

As far as Susannah was concerned, that explained why Jeremy seemed moody. Wouldn't anyone be who had been abandoned by his own mother?

"They said Tina might have the flu," Callie told him. "I don't see how the flu could put someone in Intensive Care. That sounds very weird to me." She shrugged. "But that's what they're saying." She glanced at Kate with obvious disdain as she spoke. "Of course," she added, taking Jeremy's arm and beginning to lead him over to the alcove, "they're not doctors or nurses. We should probably talk to someone who is. But first, we'll see what Tina's parents have to say, right?"

Jeremy allowed himself to be led along the hallway.

"Why do I feel like I've just been stepped on?" Kate asked, her eyes on the pair as they arrived in the alcove. Tina's parents stood up to greet them.

"She's not the most tactful person in the world," Susannah said sympathetically. "She and Jeremy make a good pair. Neither one of them is exactly a ray of sunshine."

"Yeah, but Jeremy has a good excuse." Abby's usually cheerful face was somber. "I can't imagine how it must feel to have your mother take off like Mrs. Barlow did. And leave you behind."

"Well, Callie's mother is sick," Susannah said, "so in a way, Callie's been abandoned, too. At least, she probably feels like she has."

"That's no excuse for acting like a queen addressing the peasants," Kate said. "If she thinks I'm going to curtsy when she shows up just because her father runs this place, she is crazy."

Leaving Callie and Jeremy to Tina's parents, the four took an elevator downstairs to the cafeteria.

"Now," Abby said firmly when they were all seated in the large, noisy room surrounded by tables filled with doctors and nurses in white or surgical green, "tell me what's been going on. Does Tina really have the flu?"

Susannah, with some help from Will, filled her in on the hectic arrivals of Tina and Jenkins.

Abby was shocked by the news about Jenkins. "He's not going to die, is he? I mean, it's not *that* serious, is it?" She liked Jenkins. She had talked with him a couple of times when he was doing the windows at Rehab and liked his dry sense of humor.

"He fell two and a half stories, Ab," Susannah pointed out. "His leg is a mess. The weird thing is, I think the doctors were a lot more worried about his fever than the injuries from his fall. I guess because they needed to stabilize him for surgery and his temp was getting in the way. And the other weird thing is, Callie was right about ICU almost never having flu patients. Unless they're really old or have other problems."

"If you go back to Jenkins Rue's treatment room," Kate said, "maybe you should put on a mask, so you won't get sick, too. I think I'm going to."

Susannah found that suggestion sobering. A mask? For the flu? Still, she didn't want to get sick, so maybe Kate was right.

"Anyone feel like hitting The Music Room tonight?" Abby asked as they were getting ready to leave. "Steam Engine is still there. The best band they've had in town in ages." She grinned at Susannah. "And all four of the guys are really cute. Sooz and I are going."

Susannah sighed. "Wrong. I can't go, and neither can you. I forgot, there's a fashion show rehearsal tonight. My mother's expecting us." She thought for a minute, then added, "Listen, Kate, if Tina is still too sick and can't model, would you take her place?" Kate would make a gorgeous model. With those long legs? Perfect! "The clothes are going to be gorgeous, I promise, and we each get a free outfit."

"Model? Me?" Kate envisioned the clothes she would have to wear. Probably all ruffles and lace and pastels. Or maybe those boring classic styles that Susannah's mother wore when she came to the hospital. "I don't think so."

"Oh, come on," Susannah begged. "You'd be perfect, and you know it. There's a sports-wear collection you'd look fantastic in. Please?"

Abby and Will joined in then, and the three of them, to Susannah's relief, managed to convince Kate that the fund-raising event could be fun.

"And we'll go to The Music Room tomorrow night, okay? I promise." Susannah jumped up. "Thanks, Kate. My mother will be thrilled."

"Can I have a ride home, Sooz?" Abby asked. "My mom dropped me off this morning. And can you stay over tonight?"

"Sure." Susannah had no desire to spend the evening alone in the house on the hill. Her parents had a concert to attend, and Sam wouldn't be home. Sam was never home.

"Well, I'm going back up to see how Jenkins is doing," Kate said. "Meet you up there, okay?"

"Yep." Susannah hurried off to call her mother, who would be upset to learn that Tina Montgomery was in Intensive Care, but delighted with the news that Kate had agreed to model.

On a side street in downtown Grant, an eighteen-year-old girl and her twelve-year-old brother were racing each other on Rollerblades. The boy laughed triumphantly as he easily pulled ahead of his older sister, not noticing in his glee that she had slowed considerably. She was still moving, but her gait was unsteady and her gloved hands moved up to touch her temples beneath the silver-and-black helmet she was wearing. Even if he had glanced over his shoulder, he wouldn't have been concerned by the scarlet flush on her face, thinking it had been caused by the exertion of their race.

Because he kept going, determined to stay ahead of her, he was almost a full block away when she began staggering on her skates, her hands still at her temples. Seized by a sudden coughing bout, she cried out weakly. She reached out with her hands as if to grasp something, but found nothing to grasp. Reeling dizzily, she staggered backward and fell out into the street, directly in front of an old red Ford pickup truck occupied by an elderly couple looking for the flea market. Because they weren't sure exactly where they were going, the truck was moving slowly. But the girl hit it hard, slamming backward into the passenger's door with a sharp, thwacking sound and bouncing off. She fell to the rough pavement, her hands flying out in front of her in an effort to break her fall.

The truck screeched to a halt.

The sound of its brakes brought the boy up sharply at the corner. His head whipped around. When he saw his sister's helmet lying in the street, his face drained of all color. He whirled sharply and flew back up the street on his skates to drop to his knees beside her, calling out her name.

She didn't answer.

chapter
7

Susannah and Kate arrived in Jenkins's treatment room to find the patient in the throes of a violent seizure. His body bucked wildly. His arms flailed at the air around him, and his legs, including the injured limb, kicked out frantically. The doctors and nurses at his side struggled to restrain him. A nurse who rushed to the table, hypodermic needle in hand, found it impossible to administer the sedative.

"Don't just stand there!" one of the doctors called to the pair standing openmouthed in the doorway, "get over here and help!"

Susannah got there first, and was immediately sideswiped by a flailing foot, which sent her staggering backward. Kate took her place at the table, grabbing for an ankle, seizing it, helping to hold that leg down. Susannah quickly regained her balance and pushed between two nurses who were trying valiantly to hold Jenkins's arm steady long enough for the hypo to find its target. With her help, they were able to do just that. When the medication took hold and the seizure ended, Jenkins's body finally went limp on the table.

"Take him up to X ray," one of the doctors ordered, standing back and stripping off his rubber gloves. "I want a CAT scan, stat! I've got another patient in six to look at, but I'll be up when I'm done."

As the patient was rushed from the room, Susannah looked at Kate quizzically. A brain scan? But it was Jenkins's leg that was most seriously injured.

One of the nurses noticed the look and said abruptly, "Could be the fever that caused the seizure. Maybe. But he could also have a serious head injury. We don't know how hard he hit his skull when he fell. His brain could be mush. Dr. Stiles just wants to make sure it isn't, that's all."

Susannah winced at the language. She still wasn't used to it. Kate's mother had explained to both girls that the only way some doctors and nurses could survive what they saw every day in ER was by talking and acting tough. Pretending it didn't touch them. "But it does," she had added softly. "You'd have to have a heart of stone not to be touched by it, and people with hearts of stone don't go into medicine in the first place."

"Some do," Kate had disagreed.

"If they do, they don't last," Astrid Thompson

insisted. "You have to *care* to do this every day of your life. It's essential."

With Tina already up in ICU and Jenkins on his way to Radiology, Susannah and Kate left to return to their earlier tasks, Susannah sorting insurance forms, Kate filling cabinet shelves with fresh linens.

"You didn't put a mask on before you went into that room," Kate said as they approached the nurses' station.

"Neither did you. None of the staff had them on, either, so I guess there's nothing to worry about. They're pretty careful about that kind of thing."

Kate looked dubious. "How would we know that? There hasn't been anything contagious in ER since we came on the scene. A few head colds and some flu cases, that's all."

That was true. But Susannah trusted the staff, and was positive they *would* be careful if something serious and contagious came along. No one wanted to get sick. They all saw too much of what illness could do. If masks were needed, the staff would wear them. Quickly.

Susannah and Kate had been working at their respective tasks for no more than three or four minutes when a siren died outside again, and then, almost simultaneously, another. Dropping what they were doing, they ran to the entrance to help with incoming, along with several nurses and orderlies.

The first case was a terminally ill cancer patient. He was so emaciated and unaware, Susannah could tell just by looking at him that he probably would never leave the hospital alive again. Knowing she wouldn't be needed and a little reluctant to be involved with a case that allowed no hope, she let Kate go with that stretcher to help with the paperwork, and she waited for the second incoming.

She knew the minute she saw the face that this was another case like Tina and Jenkins. The flushed skin, the eyes rolled back in the head, the coughing, all were unmistakable signs by now.

Will was on the second ambulance. He filled Susannah in as they ran down the corridor alongside of the wheeled cart carrying the patient. "Rollerblading accident," he said quickly. "Female, eighteen years old, hit a truck. No visible injuries from the collision, but whatever Tina has, this one's got it, too. Younger brother, with her at the time, said she wasn't feeling well, but he talked her into a race anyway. He's feeling guilty. Maybe you could talk to him?"

Susannah glanced behind her. A young boy, his face filled with remorse, his feet still encased in black in-line skates, sat on a chair in the hallway, his eyes never leaving the departing gurney carrying his sister. Two helmets — one silver and black, one yellow — dangled from his hands.

She was about to go to him when a third gurney burst through the doors. More nurses and orderlies ran to greet it. Medical information flew, rapid fire, from the mouths of the paramedics. Susannah didn't catch the BP or the heart rates they shouted, but she did hear, "Fifty-three-year-old male, collapsed on the job, foreman of a cleaning crew on duty in the Psych building," and then she heard, "temp, 103," and her heart sank. Another one? What was going *on*?

Susannah moved to comfort the brother of the Rollerblading accident victim.

By midafternoon, with four patients admitted who were suffering from a fever of "unexplained origin," the order had come down from above. All staff members in Emergency were to put on masks, gown, and rubber gloves before treating any patient with a fever above 101 degrees.

"We still believe it's the flu," Astrid Thompson told Susannah, Kate, and Will when she had summoned them into her office. "No lab test results yet, but they're very busy up there. I was here in 1992 when a new, vicious strain of flu hit. We weren't careful enough, and I can tell you that it's almost impossible to run a hospital with half the staff out sick. The administration isn't taking any chances this time. So masks, gloves, and gowns it is, even if you don't expect to have any physical contact with the patients. The order has come down for ICU to isolate the cases we have now, so that's being done. We're blocking off the eighth floor and sending other ICU patients to other hospitals in the complex until we know more about this fever. And if it gets too bad here," she added, looking directly at the three, "I'll have to make the treatment rooms off-limits to you girls. I can't order Will away, because he's a paramedic and has to deliver incoming. But I'd have to answer to your parents if you fell ill, Susannah." Her mouth tightened. "And I'm sure I don't have to remind you that your father is not all that happy about your volunteer work here in the first place."

Susannah nodded. She needed no reminding. Samuel Grant had had a fit when she told him what she intended to do. He thought she should be out partying, like her twin, enjoying what he called her "privileged youth" instead of "ministering to the sick" and, he had actually said, "downtrodden." Downtrodden? She had almost laughed. The richest people in the world came to Med Center. Kings, queens. Political leaders. Artists, authors, film stars, rock stars, people who had been born to wealth and could pay for the very best of everything — all flocked to Med

Center seeking a cure for one ailment or another.
Downtrodden? She didn't *think* so.

Nurse Thompson stood up. "I wouldn't want
to make an enemy of the most powerful man in
town," she told Susannah, and it seemed to the
embarrassed girl that the nurse's tone was unusually
cool. Kate probably felt the same way. Didn't
want to be a really good friend to any daughter
of Samuel Grant's. Did Will feel that way, too?
Was he afraid of her father? Afraid of who she
was? Was that why, although he was nice enough
to her, she felt this . . . this wall between them?

She had wondered if it was because she was
white. Maybe that didn't have anything to do
with it. Maybe instead it was who she was, where
she lived, what she had, and especially, who her
father was. He didn't run the hospital, but he
could certainly see to it that Astrid Thompson
lost her job if his only daughter fell seriously ill
while working in ER. He could do that. And,
Susannah had to admit reluctantly, he probably
would.

"One more thing," they were told before they
left, "you were instructed in your training that
no information about any patient leaves this hospital
with you. I realize that rule is broken so often
as to be almost useless, but in this case, I
have been told to reiterate it for you. You are not
to discuss these four new cases with anyone, is
that clear?"

All three nodded silently. Susannah remembered with a pang of guilt their discussion at lunch. All of them had discussed Tina and Jenkins with Abby. Abby would have to be warned not to repeat anything she'd heard.

"I mean this!" the head nurse stressed. "Kate, no mention of this to anyone! Do I have your promise?"

They promised.

"Good! And remember, masks, gowns, and gloves tomorrow when you come in. Although by then we'll probably have the lab results. We'll know definitely that it's the flu and we can proceed with the proper treatment. You may go now."

Abby was waiting when Susannah emerged alone into late-afternoon sunshine. Kate was still inside, waiting for the end of her mother's shift. They would go home together. Susannah felt a pang of envy. When did her family ever do anything together? Her parents went to parties and concerts and the opera; Sam attended countless parties that Susannah wasn't invited to; and she did things with her friends. But as a family, they did very little together.

Kate would stare at her in disbelief if Susannah ever said she envied Kate anything, anything at all. She who had everything.

Yeah, right.

She waited until they were in the car before repeating Nurse Thompson's warning to Abby.

"If it's just the flu," Abby said, glancing over at Susannah from the passenger's seat, "why the hush-hush? That doesn't make any sense."

"Sometimes flu becomes an epidemic. People die, sometimes," Susannah explained as she steered the Jeep carefully along the curving lanes of the ten-story parking garage. "If that's what's happening, telling people could cause a mild panic. We'd be inundated with people demanding flu shots. That wouldn't be good. I'm not even sure that ER has stocked up on a flu vaccine. Kate's mother didn't say."

"Well, they could get some fast enough. Wouldn't Grant Pharmaceuticals have it? This all sounds kind of weird to me, Susannah. Are Tina and Jenkins really that sick?"

"Yes. They wouldn't be in ICU Isolation if it wasn't serious, you know that. They took Jenkins up there right after they operated on his leg. And we've had two more cases, Abby. A girl who was Rollerblading, and an older man. They're all in ICU now. They've had practically every test and culture there is. X rays, too. And as far as I know, nobody has a clue about what's wrong with them." Susannah hadn't meant to mention the other two cases, but once the words were out of her mouth, she decided it was the right thing to say. If Abby understood that something unusual was going on, she'd understand why Emsee's administration didn't want it talked about outside of the hospital.

On a tree-lined street not far from Med Center, Susannah pulled up in front of a low, sprawling, brick ranch house.

A tall, tanned woman in bare feet, shorts, and a white T-shirt stood on the front porch, where she was watering hanging baskets of red and white flowers. Waving the brown plastic watering can toward the Jeep in greeting, she kept her other arm wrapped tightly around the dark-haired toddler she was carrying on one hip. "Hey, there!" she called. "C'mon up!" and she disappeared inside the house.

Susannah smiled as she jumped from the Jeep. Abby's mother never seemed to care if there were one or two or even six more people in her house at any given time. With six kids, a husband, and a father-in-law in residence, her attitude seemed to be, What's one or two or six more?

Inside, the O'Connor house was, as always, neat. A miracle, it seemed to Susannah, considering the crowd that occupied the bright, sunny space. The furniture might be a little worn and mismatched, the drapes a little faded, but the house was always in order. Susannah knew that everyone who lived there, including the smallest children, helped maintain that order. Even

Toothless, not quite two years old, was learning to put her toys away.

There it was again, Susannah thought with a pang, that family thing. Doing stuff together. The Grant family didn't clean house together because the Grant family didn't *clean* house. Other people were paid to do it for them.

In spite of the organized household, most mornings when Susannah arrived to pick up Abby for school or Med Center duty, her best friend was inevitably racing around the house, short, curly, dark hair like her mother's bobbing around her face as she called out, "Anybody seen my other sneaker?" (notebook, keys, purse . . .)

She was unquestionably adorable, with wide dark eyes, smooth skin, and full lips that always seemed turned up at the corners as if she were about to smile at any moment. As for the slight extra weight Abby had, it looked good on her. No sharp edges to Abby, just as there was nothing sharp-edged about her personality.

Susannah felt more at home in the O'Connor house than she ever did in her own house. Saying that aloud would have been a knife in her mother's heart, so she kept the thought to herself. Sam knew. He didn't like it, possibly because Abby was one of maybe three girls in the entire city whose heart didn't beat faster at the sight of Samuel Grant III and who didn't try to use Susannah to get to him. But he never commented at home about Susannah's preference for the O'Connor household over her own. Not while their mother was around.

They'd been in the house less than a minute when the phone rang. A boy . . . for Abby.

Knowing she'd be on the telephone at least ten minutes, Susannah took a seat on a high stool at the breakfast bar in the kitchen. With the baby in her arms and four-year-old Matthew, the only male child in the family clinging to her shorts, Mrs. O'Connor still managed to pour Susannah a glass of orange juice and set it in front of her.

"What's wrong with Mattie?" Susannah asked. "He doesn't usually trail around attached to you like that." On the contrary, the little boy was ordinarily out of the house, playing in the tree house out back or visiting a friend or frolicking in the community pool with one of his sisters.

"I think he might be coming down with a cold," Mrs. O'Connor said worriedly. "He's not himself today, are you, Mattie?" She patted his dark head.

"Don't!" he complained, rubbing his scalp. "That hurts."

His mother handed the baby to Susannah and crouched beside her small son. "Your head hurts?" She placed a hand on his forehead. It was clear from her expression that he was warmer than normal.

He nodded. "And my tummy hurts, too. Nap-time, Mommy."

Susannah's stomach lurched. The thought of sweet, adorable Matthew lying on a gurney at the hospital as ill as Tina and Jenkins made her sick.

His mother stood up, sending Susannah a worried look. "He *never* asks to go to bed. And he just got up from his nap a little while ago. I think it's time to call our doctor. I'll get this one tucked into bed first. Could you watch Toothless for a minute?"

Susannah nodded and reached for the baby, whose real name was Emma, and who finally had plenty of teeth. "You go ahead. We'll be fine."

Abby came into the kitchen a few minutes later, a pleased smile on her face. "That was Cory McGill. Wanted to know if he'd see me at The Music Room tonight. He is *so* cute. Don't you think he looks just a little bit like . . . what's wrong? You have a really weird expression on your face. And where's Mom? Wasn't she here a minute ago?"

"Nothing's wrong," Susannah answered quickly. "I mean, not really. Mattie wasn't feeling very well, so she took him up to bed, that's all."

Abby stood very still, her eyes on Susannah's face. "Sick? Mattie? Mattie is never sick. What's wrong with him?"

Susannah didn't answer. She lowered her head, pretending to be playing with the baby.

"Susannah! What's wrong with my brother?"

Susannah lifted her head. "I don't" — the words came reluctantly from Susannah's mouth — "I guess he has . . . he has a fever. But," she added hastily, "your mom thinks it's just a summer cold. I'm sure she's . . ."

But Abby was already running from the room.

chapter
8

When Abby had informed her mother about the new, puzzling cases at Med Center, Mrs. O'Connor didn't hesitate. Holding the feverish little boy by the hand, she asked Susannah and Abby to keep an eye on the other children and hurried out of the house to the family's doctor.

There was no discussion between the two girls about Nurse Thompson's order not to share with anyone the day's events at Med Center. Susannah knew Abby hadn't had a choice. If there was any chance that Mattie had something similar to what Tina and Jenkins had, the sooner he was treated, the better. Hadn't Dr. Izbecki announced in Tina's treatment room that one of the reasons she was so seriously ill was her delay in seeking treatment? Abby shouldn't take that chance with her own little brother.

Mattie and his mother were home within the hour, a relieved smile on Mrs. O'Connor's face. "Just a mild case of the flu," she told the anxious girls. "Aspirin, liquids, bed rest, and he'll be up and driving us all crazy in a day or two."

Susannah's first reaction was relief. It wasn't until she and Abby were in the car on their way to the fashion show rehearsal that she felt a new twinge of anxiety. What if the doctor was wrong? He might not know yet about Tina and Jenkins, and about the cleaning-crew foreman and the Rollerblading girl. Maybe he hadn't done all of the necessary tests on Mattie. Maybe . . .

"I know what you're thinking," Abby interrupted Susannah's thoughts as the Jeep took a sharp corner. "But Doc Alexander has been taking care of all of us since Geneva was born. That's twelve years, and he's never made a mistake yet. Sometimes all he has to do is take a look at us and he knows exactly what's wrong. Don't forget, the flu may not be what the new patients have, but it *is* going around. And that's what Mattie has, so quit worrying."

Susannah relaxed. Abby had to be right. She knew the doctor who had seen Mattie knew him well, and the O'Connors trusted him. That would have to be enough. For now.

But if Mattie wasn't better in a day or two . . .

Telling herself he *would* be, Susannah put the little boy out of her mind and drove back to Med Center.

The fashion show was being held in the Public Affairs auditorium in the Rehabilitation Hospital where Abby did much of her volunteering. One of the newer buildings, it was eight stories of rose-colored brick, with wide verandas on three sides for patients to enjoy on balmy days.

"Maybe rehearsal won't last that long," Abby said with hope as they climbed out of the Jeep, "and we can stop at The Music Room on the way home."

Susannah laughed. "You know my mother. We won't be leaving here until she's satisfied that every last detail is absolutely perfect. I have a feeling The Music Room is going to have to wait until tomorrow night. If we're lucky. If Mother doesn't like what she sees tonight, she could call rehearsals for every night this week."

To Susannah's relief and Mrs. Grant's delight, Kate showed up, ready to model. "I guess I can use a free outfit," she told Susannah with a faint grin. "And I want to do my part for Emsee. If it went out of business due to lack of funds, where would I work when I graduate from med school?"

As they went through their paces for Caroline's inspection, Susannah found herself carefully scrutinizing the faces of the other models, male and female, for any signs of illness. She saw none. A few people were coughing, but no one looked really ill. But then, Tina hadn't looked sick on Sunday night, either, and now she was in ICU.

Callie was modeling, too, but she refused to speak to Susannah and Abby.

"What's with her, anyway?" Susannah complained to Kate and Abby as they watched Callie move confidently down the runway Caroline had ordered for the show. It stretched from the stage out into the front of the auditorium. "It's like she blames us for Tina being sick. Or hasn't forgiven us for not calling her the minute Tina was brought into Emsee."

"You're disappointed that she's not speaking to you?" Kate asked, mock disbelief in her voice. "You should be ecstatic. One of the things I love most about living in Eastridge is that I don't ever, *ever* have to talk to someone like Callie Matthews. She doesn't even know I exist, and that suits me fine." Her eyes on Callie, Kate added, "How does she *do* that? Walk that way without dislocating a hip? Isn't that physiologically impossible?"

Abbie laughed. "Not for Callie. She's been walking that way since preschool. Callie and I are really too short to make good models, but you and Kate are naturals. You look perfect out there on the runway. Magazine covers, both of you. I suppose I'm not going to grow any more," Abby finished wistfully.

"No," Kate said, "you're not. And we like you just the way you are, so live with it."

Abby laughed ruefully and asked, "I don't suppose we're going to get out of here in time to stop in at The Music Room, are we?"

"Doesn't look like it. Didn't I tell you?" Susannah sighed wearily. "I'm not as disappointed as I thought I'd be. It's been a really long and pretty horrible day. I'm not sure I'd have the energy to dance."

"Sure, you would. When are you too tired to dance? But I'm beat, too. How about you, Kate? Going to go hear some music tonight?"

"Not me. I'm going to do my Naomi Campbell thing here and then I'm going home to beddy-bye, just in case tomorrow at Emsee is even worse than today was." Kate's eyes darkened. "My mom was really out of it at dinner. She only gets like that when she's worried. I know she's afraid more of that nasty stuff is going to turn up tomorrow. So," she said to Susannah, "exactly how long do you think your mother is going to keep us here?"

"I'll ask." When Susannah had pleaded their case to her mother, she agreed to let them leave, but insisted on rehearsals the following two nights.

Susannah spent Monday night at Abby's. But she didn't sleep well. Ordinarily, the cozy warmth of the O'Connor house, so different from the vast spaces of her own lavishly decorated suite at the top of Linden Hall, lulled her to sleep instantly. But after the house had stilled for the night, her mind refused to follow suit. Concern over the strange new cases at Emsee and her fears that Mattie was coming down with the same thing, in spite of what the doctor had said, kept her tossing and turning.

Abby had fallen asleep promptly, her clothes in a discarded heap on the hardwood floor, her head buried in her pillow.

Susannah finally succeeded in doing the same by reminding herself sternly that she wasn't a doctor yet, so what did *she* know? If the O'Connor family doctor, with his years of education, training, and experience, said Mattie had a simple case of the flu, then that was what he had.

In the foothills below the Grant mansion, Callie Matthews fumed. Her father had just left her room, after trying in vain to explain what his secretary Lindsay had been doing in his arms. "Perfectly innocent," he had said, sitting on Callie's bed while she paced back and forth angrily on the lush pink carpet. Her arms were folded against her chest like a shield, as if she were determined that his words would bounce off her. "Nothing happened, Callie. I love your mother, and I would never do anything to hurt her. Lindsay's sister is very sick. She's coming to Med Center for treatment, as a matter of fact. Tomorrow. I was simply trying to comfort a friend in need."

Callie wasn't listening. Her response was to toss her head stubbornly and think, Tell it to someone who cares. He could talk until his lips were purple, but she knew what she'd seen. How stupid did he think she was? He was probably just afraid she'd tell her mother. "I would appreciate it," she said icily, "if you would leave my room. I'd like to be alone."

When he left, his shoulders braced as if he expected her to throw something at his back, she still hated Med Center and she still hated every single past, present, and future Grant.

Jeremy Barlow sat alone in the dimly lit kitchen at his home and thought about how quiet the house had become since his mother left. His father called her "unconventional, undisciplined, and immature," and he said it with undisguised contempt. Maybe it was true. But his mother was *fun*. Not quiet and aloof like his father, so lost in his Very Important Work as a world-renowned cardiac surgeon. People came from all over the world to see Dr. Thomas Barlow, while his son and, for a long time, his wife, waited for him at home.

His mother hadn't been quiet. Always making some kind of noise. Laughing or talking or singing at the top of her lungs even though she wasn't very good at it, or yelling at his father or the housekeeper or the gardener or, on the phone, her mother. Some kind of noise. The house was like a tomb since she'd left.

He could have gone with her. She had asked

him to. But he'd lived in Grant all his life. What did he know about California? His friends were here, his life was here, his home . . .

And then there was the money. No small thing, his father's fortune. It paid for cars and camps and stereos and computers and clothes and parties and all those not-so-insignificant things that made life pleasant. Very pleasant. His mother was hoping to eke out a writing career in California. Everyone knew writers didn't make any money.

Jeremy didn't want to be poor. He didn't think he'd be very good at it.

So he hadn't gone. He'd stayed in Grant. But he'd never thought about how quiet the house would be without his noisy, unconventional, *fun* mother in it.

She'd done okay out there in la-la land. She'd actually sold a couple of books. She wasn't going to be poor, after all. Every once in a while she called and said, "Come on out, Jeremy, I miss you." And sounded like she meant it.

He was tempted. But the thought of leaving Grant terrified him. He wasn't good at making friends. One of his few friends was really sick. Tina. When you didn't have all that many friends, even losing one of them temporarily to sickness was depressing. What was wrong with Tina, anyway? She hadn't looked very well at The Music Room the other night. He remembered asking her if she was okay, and recalled her retorting, "Your father's the doctor, not you, Jeremy, remember?"

He hadn't been offended. Tina got like that sometimes. Her life wasn't so perfect, either. Maybe his mother was right. Maybe having money wasn't the answer to everything.

On Tuesday, there were no new cases of the nasty "flu." Every test result came back negative, leaving the illness undiagnosed.

On Wednesday, there were two new cases, one, a friend of Sam's, whose vigilant mother caught her son's fever before it went above 100 and drove him to the hospital. He was given medication and, although he wasn't seriously ill yet, dispatched quickly to Isolation on the eighth floor.

The second patient arrived by ambulance. Kate, wearing the requisite long-sleeved, pale blue coverall, plastic gloves, hood, mask, and goggles, was waiting at the door with other staff members when Will came running in with two other paramedics, pushing a wildly delirious patient on a gurney. She knew who the new patient was the minute she saw the curly, dark brown hair and the thin, silver identification bracelet on one of the flailing wrists. Damon Lawrence.

"I just saw him on Monday," Kate told Will as they ran along the corridor. "He offered me a ride. He didn't look sick."

Alarmed, Will asked, "You didn't accept, did you?"

She knew why he'd asked. The illness, whatever it was, was clearly contagious. No one knew yet exactly what the incubation period was, but it didn't take a medical genius to figure out that being in close quarters, such as the cab of a truck, with Damon on Monday would have been risky.

"No. I took the bus instead."

"Good girl."

Damon Lawrence's temperature was 104. There was an argument in the treatment room about the wisdom of dosing him with a strong antibiotic "cocktail," one of the residents arguing that it could hamper a diagnosis later, if it killed off the bacteria plaguing him before they could identify that bacteria.

"This kid can't afford to wait for cultures to come back!" Dr. Izbecki snapped. "He's on fire here. We'll worry about the consequences later. Besides, we've had no luck culturing the other cases."

The antibiotic "cocktail" was administered.

Kate knew why Damon was so sick. Because he was macho and stubborn and wouldn't have admitted he was sick until his legs would no longer carry him. With *this* sickness, that was a definite mistake.

There were other emergencies all day Tuesday

and Wednesday, but most of the staff, careful to wear the awkward, annoying, protective clothing at all times, was focused on the illness plaguing the ICU. They sutured minor and major lacerations, did X rays on victims of falls and car accidents and brawls, took blood from people with vaguer complaints such as abdominal pain and back pain and headaches, but all the while they were subconsciously awaiting another fever victim to arrive by ambulance.

At rehearsal on Tuesday and Wednesday nights, Susannah listened again for any sounds of a harsh, racking cough, and surreptitiously scanned faces for signs of a feverish flush or unusually bright eyes.

On Thursday morning, Tina Montgomery slipped into a coma.

The news circulated quickly in ER.

Susannah was horrified. Comatose? Tina was comatose? She was that close to . . . dying?

Tina Montgomery was only seventeen years old.

chapter

9

On Thursday, Susannah spent the night at Abby's again. But first, they went to The Music Room.

They said they were going because they wanted to hear Steam Engine play again. They said they were going because they wanted to dance, to be with friends, to have a good time. Hadn't they been waiting all week for this chance?

But they both knew the real reason for their need to have fun was Tina Montgomery's coma. That was too scary. Sitting around the house doing nothing would have given them too much time to think about the fact that someone their own age had suddenly been stricken by an illness so serious that she was hovering near death. That was one part of it. The other part of it was, they needed to reassure themselves that they were still healthy and very much alive and not hovering anywhere *near* death.

But what they told each other aloud was that they were going because they couldn't wait to hear the band again.

At least Mattie was getting better, Susannah told herself as she drove the Benz along the wide, tree-lined boulevards of downtown Grant. He really did have the flu, after all. And Jenkins and the Rollerblader and the cleaning-crew foreman were holding their own, although that friend of Sam's was worse, his fever spiking last night, she'd heard, to 103, and Damon Lawrence had been put on the critical list. But Mattie was okay. Something good to think about. To keep from thinking about Tina's coma.

All of the medical personnel at Memorial had been tested for any sign of the fever. They had all tested negative. So far. No one knew how long it took for the illness to develop. They would all have to be tested again. Soon.

Susannah pulled into the crowded parking lot at The Music Room, a low, sprawling, stone building situated on the far edge of a newly revitalized warehouse district. The club was distant enough from popular restaurants in that area to keep loud music from disturbing patrons.

A cavernous space that easily could have been cold, dark, and forbidding, The Music Room had been made welcoming by the clever use of soft lighting, the warm glow of burnished hardwood flooring, and round, wooden tables covered with yellow-striped cloths that fell to the floor. Candles settled in black, wrought iron candleholders, each the metal silhouette of a musician playing an instrument, were centered on each table, their flickering flames adding to the warmth.

Although the club served no meals, their specialty in snack foods was a generous selection of tiny pizzas in varying combinations of sauces, meats, and cheeses.

Susannah breathed in the spicy smell with anticipation as she and Abby entered to loud music, laughter, and chatter. Too depressed over the news about Tina to eat before they dressed at Abby's house, they'd had nothing to eat since lunch, and she was starving.

The first person she spotted out on the dance floor as they entered was her twin, Sam, as expert at dancing as he was at every other athletic feat. He was with Callie Matthews, who was wearing a sexy, slinky red dress, her hair piled on top of her head with a few undisciplined ringlets curling around her ears and on the nape of her neck. Sam laughed at something Callie said, then bent his head to give her a long, slow kiss. Callie put her arms around his neck and moved as close to him as she could.

Abby looked at the two in disgust. "Could they possibly get any closer? I see she's really devastated by her best friend's illness," Abby said with disgust. "Maybe we should go over there and console her, what do you think?"

"Can we eat first? My stomach feels like it has a hole in it. And," Susannah added sardonically, "I hope Callie realized that kiss meant nothing. I don't care how sexy it was. All Sam was saying was, I'm having a good time and I feel like kissing you. But don't call me tomorrow, I'll call you . . . maybe. If Callie is looking for commitment, she's draping herself around the wrong guy."

They took seats at one of the tables surrounding the dance floor, glancing around the softly lit, noisy room as they waited for their tray of snacks and their drinks. Susannah spotted Kate, sitting at a far table with friends. Will was there, too, talking to a pretty, dark-haired girl. In one split second, Susannah's feelings went from joy that Will was there to disappointment that he seemed unaware of her presence to jealousy of the girl he was talking to.

"He looks great in that blue shirt, doesn't he?" Abby teased, her own eyes traveling through the crowded room in search of friends. "You could ask him to dance, you know. This is the nineties, Sooz."

"I just wanted to wave to Kate," Susannah replied defensively. "And I don't *want* to dance right now. If I don't eat something, I'm going to faint. Besides," she said, glancing disconsolately once more at Kate's table, "he's busy."

Before Abby could reply, Jeremy Barlow appeared at the table. Without waiting for an invitation, he reversed a chair and plopped down in it, resting his chin on the back. "So, how's Tina doing? You guys know what's wrong with her yet? Give! No point in having friends who slave all day at Med Center if you're not going to tell all."

Susannah realized immediately that he didn't know about the coma. His mood would have been very different if he'd been told. He must not have talked to Tina's parents yet.

"Ask your father." Abby's tone was light, but her eyes showed her discomfort. Susannah knew she felt guilty about not telling Jeremy the truth. But that wasn't for them to do. "He probably knows more about Tina's case than we do."

Jeremy shook his head. "Not true. He spends most of his time up there in his ivory tower in Cardiac/Pulmonary, away from ER. Anyway," he added more seriously, "Tina's a friend of mine. Callie and I are worried about her."

"Yeah, right," Abby said dryly. "We noticed." She stared pointedly at Callie and Sam, still dancing to a loud, fast beat from the band onstage at the front of the room. "Paralyzed with grief, that girl."

"We came here to take our minds off it, that's all," Jeremy retorted, offended. "Can't just sit around waiting to hear something. Everyone's talking about how sick Tina is, but no one *knows* anything. I figured you guys would."

"Well, we don't," Abby said, and then the waitress arrived with their snacks and drinks. Abby plucked from the tray four miniature pizzas with a Coke, and a folded yellow-and-white-striped paper napkin. "Anyway, I was at Rehab all day."

Jeremy turned his attention to Susannah, just as she had known he would. Dreaded he would. She didn't like lying. And Jeremy *was* a good friend of Tina's. But Nurse Thompson had been very explicit in her instructions. "You know about hospital rumors, Jeremy," she said. "Your father's a doctor. You must hear stuff all the time. That doesn't mean it's true."

"Doesn't mean it's not, either. Come on, Susannah, I'll find out sooner or later, anyway. Is Tina going to be okay?"

"I'm just an uneducated volunteer. What do I know?"

Jeremy might have continued to argue, but a friend of Susannah's came to ask her to dance. Although she was still hungry, she would have danced with Count Dracula himself at that point to get away from Jeremy's questions. She accepted the invitation and left the table.

She could feel Jeremy's puzzled eyes on her back as she moved away.

She waved at Sam as they passed him on the dance floor. He nodded, his face flushed with exertion. He was dancing with a different girl now, a tall redhead, which didn't surprise Susannah. His eyes seemed unusually bright, but she told herself that was from the exercise. Sam threw himself into his dancing, the same way he did everything else. And he *was* good.

Her partner, a stocky boy named Paul, commented on the band as they passed the stage. "They're really great, aren't they?"

Nodding enthusiastically, Susannah glanced at the four onstage. The boy on lead guitar, standing directly behind the microphone, caught her eye. He grinned, a lazy, confident smile that lit up his eyes and sent an unmistakable message to Susannah. It said very clearly, I like what I'm looking at.

Susannah didn't look away. Instead, she smiled back. Why not? Will Jackson certainly hadn't acknowledged her existence tonight, and this guy was *very* cute. Tall and thin, his jeans slung low on his hips, a white T-shirt on slightly stooped shoulders.

He had the kind of lean, bony looks she liked. His hair was long, to his shoulders, and dark and wavy, but very clean, shining under the stage lights. Susannah was an "eye person." She really believed that you could tell a lot about a person if you just checked out their eyes. His were incredible. Warm and intelligent, dark brown like Will's, but with glints of gold and amber in them. Or maybe that was just the reflection of the stage lights.

Still, they were great eyes. It wasn't easy to look away from that boldly interested gaze, and she didn't. Not until she could no longer see him without craning her neck.

She said hi to Will and Kate as she passed their table and added casually, "Come over and say hi to us when you get a minute."

But she knew they wouldn't. Kate had an unspoken rule about socializing. She had never mentioned it aloud, but Susannah wasn't stupid. When Kate went places with Susannah and Abby, she never asked to bring along any of her school or neighborhood friends. And when she was with *those* friends, someplace where Susannah and Abby happened to be, Kate acted like they hardly knew each other.

Susannah had never said anything about it. She knew it was harder for Kate, who had to go back home to Eastridge after she'd been out socializing with white kids. Maybe Will felt the same way, since he'd never once asked her to dance or to a movie or a party. Abby kept saying he wanted to, she could tell, but that he was afraid, because of who she was. "Your father would have a stroke if he saw you with Will and you know it. So does Will," had been her explanation.

It was all very confusing to Susannah. Sometimes when Will looked at her, she thought she saw interest in his eyes. But nothing ever happened. So maybe, although she was usually good at reading eyes, this time she was reading them wrong. Which meant that Abby was misreading the signs, too, and Will just wasn't interested.

Abby would have laughed and said, "Me? Wrong? Never happen!"

But Will Jackson wasn't approaching the table to ask Susannah Grant to dance, was he?

No, he wasn't.

And that guitar player, who still had his eyes on her, she noticed when she glanced toward the bandstand, was obviously interested.

To Susannah's immense relief, Jeremy had left their table. She saw him sitting with Callie Matthews and two other girls from Tina's crowd. They were all talking earnestly, and she saw Callie glance over her shoulder toward Susannah and Abby with venom in her eyes.

She's mad because we won't tell her anything about Tina, Susannah thought. But we can't tell her, because we don't know anything except that she's in a coma. And *that* we can't tell her. That terrible news has to come from Callie's parents.

Abby and two of her friends took advantage of

the band break to go to the rest room. Susannah was sitting at the table alone, plucking absentmindedly at the music staff candleholder, when the tall, thin guitarist with the amber eyes appeared in front of her.

"Mind if I join you?" he asked, and didn't sit down until Susannah, who wasn't the least bit surprised to see him there, said, "No, I don't mind."

His name was Zack Ballou. The band, Steam Engine, had been his idea, and he really liked Grant, Massachusetts. "What I've seen of it, anyway," he added quickly. "We don't leave here until around two A.M. usually, so we all sleep late, and then we rehearse afternoons. Doesn't leave a lot of time for sightseeing. Pretty town, though. Sort of Beaver Cleaverish. Big trees, nice houses, wide streets. People seem friendly. We sneaked in a quick tour of Med Center. My aunt's a nurse. When she heard I was coming here, she made me promise I'd take a look at it. It's pretty impressive."

"I work there," Susannah said with pride. Deciding that had sounded a little smug, she quickly added, "I mean, I volunteer. In ER."

"Must be exciting. The place is enormous. So many different hospitals. If I ever get sick, I'll know where to come. So," he said, leaning forward and edging his chair a little closer to Susannah's, "going to be a doctor someday, are you?" He smiled. "You're going to be really busy. Every guy in the city will be pounding on your door. They'll quit working out, quit eating right, hoping they'll get sick just so they can see you."

If it was a line, it worked. Susannah smiled back. Most guys would have asked her if she planned to be a nurse, not a doctor. "I haven't decided. Maybe." Abby danced past, grinned, gave her the thumbs-up sign. Susannah hoped Zack hadn't seen.

While the band took its break, a disc jockey took over. The current tune was a slow one. Zack stood up and held out his hand to Susannah. She took it and let him lead her to the dance floor, hoping Will Jackson was watching from his table.

"And your name is?" Zack Ballou asked, which answered one question that had been on Susannah's mind: Whether or not he knew who she was. So far, her dating experiences had involved two kinds of guys: the ones who were terrified of her father and treated her like something breakable, which she hated, and the guys who thought that getting in good with Samuel Grant's daughter might be a smart move.

But Zack didn't even know her name. Probably had never even heard of Samuel Grant II. Just in case he had, she gave him her first name only. Then she gave him a brief history of Grant and Emsee.

"I've been hearing rumors all night about that place," he said. "Something about a new flu. Know anything about that?" Before she could think of how to avoid answering the question, he added, "I don't want to sound like a wimp, but we can't afford to get sick. After we're done here, we're on our way to Vegas. One of our better gigs. Our agent promised us the hotel room would actually have hot water and room service. So if there's something catching going around, we should probably know about it."

"It's nothing to worry about," she said with more conviction than she felt. "I really don't know much about it myself." Except that one of the victims is now in a coma, she thought, and felt a twinge of guilt about not warning him. But she had her orders.

"No problem. I was just curious. If you find out anything more, let me know, okay?"

They talked then about his travels and what it was like to be on the road so much. He said it was hectic, but fun. "Sometimes. We've traveled out of the country once in a while. Those gigs are hard, lugging all of our gear and not having a clue about where anything is. But they're the most interesting, too. I've learned more on those trips than I ever learned in geography in school.

Problem is, we haven't hit it big with an album yet, so some of the places we've played have been pretty sleazy." He smiled down at Susannah. "Grant's one of the best, by the way. At least here, we can drink the water. Can't do that in B.Y.O.B.W. places."

Susannah glanced up inquiringly. "B.Y.O.B.W.?"

He laughed. "Bring your own bottled water. We've been sick a couple of times. In other countries, mostly. Had to cancel some gigs, which we all hate to do, because we were laid out in the hotel room with what the local doctors called 'stomach distress.' Distress is right. The last time was the worst. Man, were we laid low! Now we carry our own water with us."

Abby danced by again, this time in the arms of Cory McGill, the boy who had telephoned her on Monday. Then Sam passed, dancing with an unsmiling Kate. Susannah was surprised. She knew Kate didn't think much of Sam. She'd made remarks from time to time, calling him, among other things, "a party animal." Susannah had retorted once, "That doesn't mean he's not a nice guy."

"Doesn't mean he is, either," Kate had replied.

It struck Susannah now that Sam's face was beet red. Probably from dancing too hard. But his eyes seemed unusually bright, too.

It's all those cases of the flu or whatever we've been seeing, she told herself, returning her attention to Zack. I'm starting to see that same illness in everyone. First Mattie, who only had the flu after all, and now my own brother, who is as healthy as Schwarzenegger. I'm being silly.

But the following morning, she changed her mind.

chapter
10

In an inexpensive motel on the outskirts of Grant, Zack Ballou lay on the thin plaid bedspread thinking about the quiet, pretty girl with the brilliant smile.

"You know who that girl was? The one you danced with?" Skeet, the keyboard player, had asked Zack on the way home.

"Yeah. Her name's Susannah."

"Susannah *Grant*, man. That name ring a bell? Think a minute, Zack. Where *are* we?"

"We're in Grant, Massachusetts." Zack, driving the rental car, had turned his head toward Skeet. "So? Are you telling me that girl has an entire city named after her?"

"That's what I'm sayin', man. Her ancestors founded this place. Her old man practically owns the whole town. Remember that big white house we saw at the top of the hill when we were checking out Med Center? You said it looked like one of those mansions we saw in Beverly Hills when we were meeting with our agent in L.A., remember? We thought it might be a resort."

Zack nodded.

"Well, that's where your Susannah *lives*, Zack. While you, my friend," Skeet added with a grin, "live on the road. You got no home. Well, I mean, you got a family in Sacramento, but you're never there, am I right? You're a vagabond with luggage and guitar, making music, eating in fast-food joints, and sleeping in cheap motels in places where we can't even drink the water. My pitiful little brain tells me that's not what this girl's parents have in mind for her."

I didn't *ask* her to marry me, Zack thought, rolling over restlessly on the bed. She's nice, she's friendly, smart and pretty, and that smile could light up this entire city. But no entanglements, that's the rule. *My* rule. The band's rule. We haven't worked as hard as we have to ruin the whole thing by letting some female come along and carry one of us off, leaving the others in the lurch. Susannah Grant's parents could quit worrying.

Besides, there was something a lot more important to think about. That new sickness rumored to be plaguing Med Center could do a lot more damage to the band than Zack Ballou losing his heart to Susannah Grant. He'd heard there were only six cases. Six was too many, as far as he was concerned. Six meant it was probably contagious. Getting sick was *not* in Steam Engine's master plan. On their last trip out of the country, Skeet had fallen ill only an hour or two before stage time. Too late to try and find a replacement, even if they had spoken the language, which they hadn't.

Their performance wasn't the same without Skeet. Fortunately, the audience hadn't seemed to notice. Too busy yakking. He hated audiences like that. It had been one of those nights he hated, when no one was paying attention. So Skeet's absence hadn't ruined their careers. But another time, in a better club . . . maybe in someplace like Grant, Massachusetts, with a more attentive audience, the absence of one musician could wreck everything.

And there just might be something floating around this city that could strike them all down if they weren't careful. Or lucky.

That girl . . . Susannah . . . she was someone important? Rich? Someone whose parents would lock her in her room forever if they caught her with an itinerant musician? Too bad.

Still, he just might call her or try to see her again. She worked at Med Center. Maybe she could keep him up-to-date on whatever was going around, making people sick.

Well, of course that's why you want to see her again, a sarcastic inner voice scoffed. It has nothing to do with the fact that she's one of the prettiest, nicest females on the planet, right?

Zack closed his eyes. But for just a few more

seconds before he fell asleep, he silently played in his head the last tune he and Susannah had danced to.

At Med Center, on the eighth floor of Grant Memorial in a small room with an Isolation sign on the door, Damon Lawrence, the newest patient to arrive at ICU, went into cardiac arrest.

The green jagged line continuously zigzagging across the screen on a monitor behind the patient's head became instead a steady, flat line.

An alarm sounded at the ICU nurses' station.

Two of the nurses on the floor were already wearing gowns, with masks hanging around their necks. They were on their feet and inside the room in seconds, while other nurses hurriedly donned the proper gear before entering.

The first nurse to reach the patient, snatched up a wrist and quickly called out to the nurses who arrived a second later, "No pulse! Get a crash cart in here, stat! It's right outside! And call Cardiology! Get Barlow. If he's not in the hospital, call his service!"

Feet ran to obey. The nurse was administering CPR to no avail when a white-jacketed resident, looking decidedly weary, arrived alongside the red wheeled crash cart. Quickly realizing that the CPR wasn't doing the trick, he began shouting orders for medication to be injected into the already established IV lines, simultaneously smearing the cart's electrical paddles with gel. The nurses obeyed his orders smoothly, efficiently, as if they'd been choreographed. One inserted the requested amount of medication into an IV line, then quickly stepped away from the bed as the doctor shouted, "Clear! Give me one-fifty!"

The paddles smacked down upon Damon's bare chest.

All eyes went to the monitor.

Nothing. No response.

"I'm gonna hit him again!" the resident said tersely. "Give me two hundred!"

The nurse tending the crash cart moved a dial.

"Clear!"

The paddles smacked downward a second time.

Again, there was no response.

"This kid shouldn't be *dying!*" the resident, a very young man, exclaimed. "He's what . . . sixteen, seventeen?"

"But we don't know what he's *got!*" a young nurse said unnecessarily.

"Two-fifty!" the doctor ordered. "Where the hell is Barlow, anyway?"

"Couldn't raise him. Left a message with his service. If he's in town, he'll call. I put out a call for anyone from Cardiology. Someone's probably on the way."

"Well, they'd better hurry. One more time. Give me three hundred! Clear!"

This time, Damon responded. "I've got a pulse," one of the nurses declared, relief heavy in her voice. "BP one hundred over fifty. He's with us again."

The green line returned to its zigzag pattern again.

There was a palpable easing of tension in the room.

The doctor returned the paddles to the crash cart. "Even if Barlow approved of cracking open chests for open-heart massage, which he doesn't," he said, looking down at the patient, whose chest rose and fell evenly now, "I wouldn't have done it. Whatever he's got, I wouldn't want to be the one to let it loose. Better it stays inside him, where it belongs. Besides," he added wryly with typical hospital humor, "I've never even cracked a walnut without crushing the thing to smithereens."

As the resident and all but one of the nurses left the room, he asked more seriously, "Any luck getting his fever down?"

"Oh, we can get it down. That's no problem. It's *keeping* it down that's got us stumped. It goes right back up again. We're still dosing all of them with antibiotics, but if you ask me, they need a different course of treatment. Just don't ask me what."

Frowning, the young resident left to continue the nap interrupted by the emergency.

When Dr. Barlow, Chief of Cardiology at ER, finally called from the country club where he'd been having dinner, he was told he wasn't needed, after all, and that the patient was stable and resting as comfortably as could be expected.

Susannah stayed at Abby's house again. When she arrived home on Friday morning to change her clothes, her family was gathered in the sunny breakfast room. Her first reaction as she waved casually in her twin's direction was that he looked really terrible. His face was flushed, and his hand shook noticeably as he reached for a pitcher of juice. Instead of responding to her wave, he began to cough.

"What's the matter with you?" she asked abruptly, moving over to stand behind his chair. "I thought you looked weird last night at The Music Room." She glanced at Caroline. "Mother? Sam's sick."

"I am not!" he protested between coughs. "Mind your own business." The coughing stopped. Clearing his throat, he added, "Like you were really paying attention to *me* last night. How many times did you dance with that musician? Three? Four?"

Caroline glanced up in alarm. "Musician? What musician? Good heavens, Susannah, you're not dating a musician, are you?" The tone of her voice made it clear that the word "musician" could easily have been synonymous with "ax murderer."

"Never mind, Mother. Did you hear what I said? Look at Sam! He's sick, isn't that obvious?"

"Sick?" Caroline shook her head. "Don't be silly, darling, your brother is never ill. Neither are you. Nettie Montgomery tells me I have the healthiest children in the world. You know," she added in a confidential tone, as if she were sharing a secret, "her Tina is quite ill."

"I know, Mother. I work in ER, remember? I was there when they brought her in."

"You volunteer, dear." Caroline paused, then added anxiously, "You wouldn't want people thinking we've sent you out to *work*."

"Damn nuisance," Samuel Grant said, "that Montgomery girl getting sick just now. Leonard was supposed to return to South America on Friday, finish up the business with that promising new herb our field people have discovered. Could be a new miracle drug, from the early reports we've received. I can't very well send him when his daughter is in the hospital."

"That was very thoughtless of Tina," Susannah said, annoyed that all attention had shifted away from the physical condition of her twin. "She should have consulted with you before she developed a fever of one hundred and three."

"Susannah!" Caroline said quickly. "You're being rude."

"And *he's* ignoring me as usual! So are you, Mother!" Susannah slapped a hand across Sam's brow before he could stop her. He pushed the hand away immediately, but Susannah had already felt the heat from his skin. "Mother, he's burning up! I told you he was sick."

Smoothly, calmly, Caroline stood up and walked over to her son. She repeated the touch on the brow, and when she pulled her hand away, said slowly, "Why, Sam, you do seem to be warm."

"I just got out of the sauna," he said impatiently, tossing his napkin aside and jumping to his feet. Susannah was sure he was lying. Beginning to cough again, her brother brushed past her and hurried from the room, calling over his shoulder as he left, "Quit treating me like a baby, okay? I am *not* sick!"

"He is *so*!" Susannah insisted, staring at her mother as if to say, What are you going to do about this? "Look, the reason Tina is so sick now is, she didn't get herself to a doctor soon enough. That's what Izbecki said. You don't want Sam to end up in Emergency, too, do you?"

"Izbecki?" her mother asked, frowning. "You don't have any friends named Izbecki, do you, dear? Is that the musician Sam mentioned?"

"He's a doctor, Mother."

"I'll handle this," Samuel said, rising. "No need for you girls to worry your pretty heads about it."

"Mother isn't a girl," Susannah said in exasperation. An overwhelming need to scream in frustration was sweeping over her. "She's a woman."

She might as well have saved her breath. "Well, she's right about one thing," her father continued as he turned to leave the room. "Sam is never sick. Healthy as a horse."

"Why do people always say that?" Susannah cried. "Even horses get sick!"

Ignoring her, her father continued, "I'm sure he's just been overdoing it a little, the way boys his age tend to do. I did it myself, I must admit. I'll have a talk with him."

"Make him see a doctor!" Susannah insisted, thinking of Tina lying on that gurney, her body consumed by fever.

Her father's face reddened slightly. He stared at her coolly, remarking, "Surely your volunteer duties at Med Center haven't equipped you to make medical diagnoses, have they, Susannah? Perhaps you should leave that to the proper professionals for the time being." He managed a small, tolerant smile. "At least until you've graduated from high school."

"Ooh!" Susannah cried, furious, and whirled on her heel to run out of the room and stomp upstairs. She didn't stop at Sam's room to see how he was. What was the point? Even if she decided he was at death's door, no one would listen to her.

She changed into white jeans and a white silk blouse, rolled the sleeves up to the elbow, thrust her pale hair up into a thick, bouncy ponytail, and left the house without saying another word to anyone.

In his own suite of rooms, Sam Grant lay on an upholstered sofa near the window, which was wide open. He was hoping the fresh morning air would clear his head, cool his body, which felt like he *was* in the sauna.

He was *never* sick. Never. Everyone else got colds and the flu, never him.

He hated *this*, whatever it was. It sure felt rotten. He couldn't stop coughing, and his head was about to explode.

He knew how to handle it, though, even if he didn't know what it was. Tough it out. Like the old man was always telling him, "You give in to adversity, son, that makes you a loser. There is nothing you can't overcome, as long as you don't knuckle under."

He wasn't going to knuckle under. But he sure did feel like he was bending a little.

With a great deal of effort, Sam pulled himself upright on the sofa and breathed deeply of the morning air. The result was a coughing spell that doubled him in half. When it had finally passed, he stood up, swiped at his watering eyes with the back of a hand, and moved unsteadily to the medicine cabinet in his bathroom. There, he withdrew a bottle of aspirin and downed two with a glass of water.

An hour later, he decided he felt better, just as he'd expected, and left the house to drive down into Grant in his van to see who was having the most fun. That group was the one he would join.

Another challenge won, he thought with satisfaction. Now, if he could just stop this stupid coughing. . . .

At the O'Connor house, Susannah was delighted to see that Mattie was feeling much better.

"I heard there are more cases at Emsee," Mrs. O'Connor commented quietly when Susannah moved on into the kitchen to wait for Abby to gather all of her things together. "How many?"

Susannah remembered Nurse Thompson's warning. "I . . . I'm not sure."

Abby's mother smiled. "Yeah, you are. Abby wouldn't tell me, either. You're not supposed to, right? And as long as I know Mattie's going to be okay, I guess I should quit worrying." She turned away to pile breakfast remains into the refrigerator, then turned back to Susannah. "But I do have other kids, you know. If there's something nasty going around, parents in Grant should be informed."

"I'm sure if it was anything nasty, you'd be told," Susannah said with more confidence than she felt. Seeing once again Tina's flushed face and wild eyes on the gurney, she suffered a pang of guilt. But orders were orders.

Abby came in then, wearing a Boston Red Sox sweatshirt, baggy white shorts, and work boots with thick white socks. Her face was flushed, her curly, dark hair askew. But she was always flushed after her mad rush around the house gathering her things together, so Susannah knew the high color had nothing to do with illness.

On the way to Med Center, she told Abby about Sam.

"I noticed last night, when he was dancing with Kate, that he looked a little weird," Abby agreed. "Like he was feverish or something. But then I figured it was just that I was worried about Mattie. So I forgot about him and concentrated on you and that guitarist instead. He really is pretty cute, Sooz. I planned to grill you about him last night, but the minute I hit that bed, I was out like a light. Are you going to see him again?"

"Maybe." Susannah smiled slyly, thinking of Zack's eyes on hers. "I do so appreciate good music, don't you?"

Abby laughed. "Oh, I do! I do!"

chapter
11

—◁╲◁╲◁╱╲◁╱╲◁╱╲◁╱╲◁—

Callie Matthews arrived at Med Center early Friday morning.

She almost turned around and left when she glimpsed two nurses on their way into a treatment room. They looked like astronauts in weird blue coveralls, hoods, gloves, and goggles! She knew what that clothing was. It was protective gear, protection against contamination of some kind. Against contamination from *Tina*, she'd bet. And the others who had what Tina had. Was it really that dangerous?

She wasn't supposed to have seen the nurses, she knew that, too. She'd bet her sports car that no one outside of the hospital was supposed to see them. They probably didn't put on their space gear until just before they entered a treatment room, and then only if the patient was sick like Tina. They certainly weren't hanging around near any entrances dressed like that. If they were, the whole town would know that someone at Med Center was contagious. And the whole town *didn't*. Not yet.

116

The protective clothing scared Callie. No one had told her Tina was sick with something that *dangerous*. No one would even tell her how Tina *was*, and she hadn't been allowed near ICU. Tina's parents were so vague. They just kept saying, "She's holding her own, she's holding her own." What did *that* mean?

If Tina had something dangerous and contagious, Callie wondered as she slipped inside an elevator, why hasn't Dad told me about it? Isn't he worried that I'll get it, too? I'm Tina's best friend!

Her father hadn't said a word to her about any dangerous illness at Med Center. He came home very late from the hospital every night, ate a quiet dinner with his wife in their bedroom, and went to bed. Every morning, he left the house earlier than he had the day before. This morning, she had noticed dark circles under his eyes. Her mother had them, too, but that was because of her illness. Her father wasn't ill.

She wasn't on her way up to the tenth floor to apologize for the way she'd acted when he tried to explain about Lindsay. Pigs would fly first. She was there because she'd gone over the limit on one of the credit cards and she wanted him to fix it. There was this divine black dress at a little shop near Med Center. She had to have it. He owed her that much, at least.

That snake Lindsay wasn't at her desk again.

But her jacket wasn't hanging on the coatrack, either, and something about the desk looked different. It was so clean. As if . . . hope rose in Callie's chest . . . as if no one worked there. Maybe, just maybe, her father had actually fired the woman. If he had, maybe she'd think about forgiving him. Not right away, of course. But sometime.

She went straight to the door of her father's office, but her hand on the knob was stopped by the sound of voices from inside. A voice she didn't recognize sounded angry, while her father's was calm, perfectly rational, and very determined.

"We have the finest lab in the world on these premises," he was saying in response to an angry remark that Callie hadn't grasped. "They'll get to the bottom of this. You're overreacting, Doctor Davis. I'm sure this is nothing more than the flu. A new strain of it, maybe, but still, just the flu. I understand there's a lot of it going around. I have also been told that several of the patients took their own sweet time seeking treatment, which is probably why they're so ill."

"The preliminary lab tests on two of the patients came back negative for influenza," the angry voice retorted. "It is *not* the flu, Matthews. We've got six cases now. The Montgomery girl, Jenkins Rue, the girl who was Rollerblading, the cleaning-crew foreman, Damon Lawrence, who is critically ill, and another boy his age. We could have more at any second. We don't even know what those six have in common. Five of them are young. But one of them is fifty-three years old."

Callie pictured her father leaning back in the huge, brown leather chair that she loved to sit in and twirl around. He probably had a look of satisfaction on his face, knowing he was far more important than the doctor standing in front of him. "Send your cultures over to the lab at Grant Pharmaceuticals. It's better equipped than ours. When you have those results, we'll talk again."

But the doctor wasn't so easily dismissed. "Matthews, I'm telling you, we're going to have more cases. This stuff is clearly contagious, and if it turns out to be influenza, I'll turn in my stethoscope. Med Center has a couple of social events scheduled on the grounds. Gathering a lot of people together here now is not a good idea. And we should be getting the word out that there's something nasty going around. May I just remind you that the Lawrence boy arrested last night, and the Montgomery girl is comatose?"

Alone in the hallway, her ear pressed to the heavy wooden door, Callie gasped in shock. Comatose? Tina? Tina was in a coma? "At death's door," that's what her father had called a coma, more than once. Tina was at death's door, and no one had told her? Her father *knew*? He knew, and he hadn't said a word?

Her father's voice was louder, clearer. He must have risen from his chair in anger. "Get the word out?" She knew *that* tone of voice. It meant he was taking her car keys, she was grounded, her allowance was being cut in half, and she'd damn well better get her grades up or she wouldn't leave the house for a year. He didn't use that tone often, but when he did, there was no budging him. Who knew that better than she?

"Get the word out?" he repeated, his voice rising steadily. "You're talking publicity, Doctor Davis? Is that what you're suggesting?"

"I'm suggesting that we warn this community that a nasty illness is making the rounds in Grant and that we don't yet know what it is or how dangerous."

"Well, now, there's a productive suggestion. Let's panic the entire city. Let's spread the word, far and wide, that Med Center is not a safe place to be just now. The resulting bad publicity ought to be an enormous help in getting us the funds we need for the new burn unit wing. Get the word out? If we do that, Doctor, this entire facility, all eighteen buildings, will empty out faster than a movie theater after someone has shouted 'fire.'"

He *knew* Tina was in a coma, Callie thought, sickened.

"Funds?" There was astonishment in the doctor's voice. "You're making this about money?"

"Everything is about money. Where do you think this medical complex would be without money, Doctor? Where would your salary come from? And the expensive equipment you doctors think of as medical toys? However, just in case you find me callous and uncaring, after your telephone call to me, I *did* speak with the Chief of Staff on this matter. I don't mind telling you, the consensus is that you're an alarmist."

"I'm alarmed. I admit that. You should be, too," Dr. Davis said.

"It wasn't wise of you to go over the Chief's head and come to me, Doctor. You would never have had access to this office if my secretary wasn't out on personal business today. A family illness. Now, if you'll excuse me . . ."

Callie's heart twisted bitterly. He hadn't fired Lindsay, after all. She just wasn't in today. She'd be back at her desk on Monday.

"There *will* be more cases," the doctor responded angrily. "And this is an illness that needs immediate treatment if more serious complications like the ones we have in ICU are to be avoided." His angry words were moving dangerously close to where Callie was huddled in hurt and anger outside the door. The doctor was leaving.

She darted sideways, hiding behind a tall, potted plant.

When the doctor, his stride furious, had disappeared inside the elevator, she left, too. The last person in the world she felt like talking to now was her treacherous, traitorous father, who could have, *should* have, warned her that her best friend was ill with something so dangerous, people had to put on protective clothing before they went near her. And how could he not have told her that Tina was in a coma?

She had nothing to say to him.

Fuming, Callie went straight home and talked her mother into giving her a different credit card. Then she went shopping.

She would wear the black dress to The Music Room that night. If she was going to catch what Tina had and maybe become comatose, too, she might as well have as much fun as she could first.

It did occur to Callie, as she drove home with the sexy black dress lying in a large pink box on the bucket seat beside her, that if she hadn't caught the disease or whatever it was from Tina by now, maybe she wasn't *going* to. Maybe she was immune or something. She put the back of her right hand to her forehead. No fever there.

No, she probably wasn't going to get it.

But she still might as well have as much fun as she could.

On Friday morning, Zack called Susannah at ER to ask if she was coming to The Music Room that night. She was surprised and pleased to get the call. But as she talked on the phone in the hall, she was painfully aware of Will standing off to one side. She knew she was being silly. He couldn't possibly know who she was talking to. Besides, why would Will care? She told herself that she was keeping her voice low only because this was, after all, a hospital.

And she told Zack that yes, she was planning on coming to hear them play that night, that she would have come back sooner but she'd been too busy.

"Great!" he said, sounding really pleased. "See you tonight. Save me a dance, okay?"

"Absolutely."

Watching Susannah, Will sensed, with a sharp pang of envy in his chest, that Susannah was talking to a guy. Probably that guitarist from The Music Room. He'd seen her dancing with the musician. Had come very close to jumping from his chair and walking over to ask her to dance himself. But he couldn't do it. He wasn't sure why. It wasn't because she was white. He had plenty of white friends, some of them girls, many of whom he wouldn't have hesitated to ask to dance.

But Susannah was different. And it wasn't her money, or the fact that her father practically owned the entire town. She wasn't a snob, and he was convinced she didn't have a prejudiced bone in her body. It was something else. Maybe it was because he sensed that any relationship between the two of them wouldn't be just a casual, friendly thing. He had a strong, gut feeling that it would go deeper than that. And even if he *could* ever get past her parents, there wasn't any room in his life for that kind of relationship right now. Wouldn't be for a long time. He had plans.

They were friends. And until he'd seen her dancing with that musician, he'd told himself that would be enough. Lying, of course, but it had worked pretty much.

Maybe tonight he would ask her to dance. One dance did not a relationship make. Besides, it would drive him nuts if she danced with that musician all night long.

But that night at The Music Room, just as Will was working up his courage to leave his chair and move swiftly to the table where Susannah, looking very pretty in a bright blue sundress that matched her eyes, sat with Abby and Jeremy Barlow and a few other friends, something happened to stop him.

What stopped him was the way Susannah was watching her twin brother Sam, out on the dance floor with Callie Matthews. The number was a fast one, and they were dancing so well together, other dancers had moved off to the sidelines to watch them. Susannah should have been smiling, as everyone else was. But she wasn't smiling, Will noticed. Her eyes on Sam were concerned, and there was a worried frown on her face.

Picking up on her expression, Will stayed in his chair and switched his attention to Sam. He understood, then, why Susannah looked worried. Sam looked terrible. His face was too flushed, his eyes too bright, and several times during the dance his hand went to his mouth to cover a cough.

While other people watching saw nothing but some awesome dancing, Will had enough experience in his work as a paramedic to recognize illness when he saw it.

They hadn't had any new cases of the fever for the past two days. Will thought, with a stab of sympathy for Susannah, that that was about to change. Because something was very wrong with Samuel Grant III.

Sam, missing a step, stumbled, and was more startled by the misstep than his audience was. Oh, man, his overheated brain thought, this is not good. This is not good at all. He continued to dance, his arms and legs moving automatically to the upbeat music. But the coughing was getting worse, and his head felt like he was dancing on *it*, instead of on his feet.

Will stood up. Susannah did the same.

Seized by a sudden, violent coughing spasm, Sam stopped dancing, putting both hands to his mouth.

Callie, her feet still moving, regarded him with a mixture of concern and annoyance. "What's wrong?"

Susannah began to move forward from one side of the room, Will from the other, both heading for the dance floor.

Sam's hands reached out blindly for something to grasp. He turned his head, his fever-bright eyes meeting Susannah's. She thought she saw him shrug helplessly. Then his knees buckled and he slid slowly, still coughing, to the floor. He landed first on his knees, remaining that way for several seconds.

Callie stopped dancing.

Susannah ran to her brother's side. Will arrived at the same moment.

But they weren't in time to stop Sam from toppling forward, landing face first on the burnished hardwood floor.

His eyes were open. But he wasn't moving.

chapter
12

Susannah fell to her knees beside Sam, calling his name.

Shouting for someone to call 911, Will, too, knelt. Gently, carefully, he rolled Sam over onto his back, loosened the collar of his light blue shirt, and took his pulse. "Get a wet cloth!" he ordered.

Kate, hurrying over to join them, turned instead and ran for the rest room.

"Somebody get me a big glass of water!" was Will's second order.

Callie obeyed, but she was so stunned, she didn't move as quickly as Kate had. How could Sam be sick? She'd known Sam Grant all of her life and she couldn't remember one single time, except for the chicken pox that they all had, when he'd been anything less than physically perfect. They'd been having such a great time, with everyone standing around watching them dance. Although now that she thought about it, Sam hadn't looked that great. She'd thought he was just flushed from dancing. Where was her brain these days? How could she not have picked up on the fact that he was getting sick, like Tina? Stupid, stupid! And because she hadn't been paying attention, she'd been breathing in his germs the whole time they were dancing!

But . . . she hadn't caught it from Tina. So maybe she wouldn't catch it from Sam, either.

Susannah leaned over her brother and patted his flushed, scarlet face with the cold cloth Kate had brought her. Fighting tears, she murmured a stready stream of words, "Sam, you idiot, why didn't you listen . . . I told you something was wrong . . . you're not stupid, you had to know you were sick . . . what is the *matter* with you, anyway? . . . oh, God, I've got to call Mother, she's going to be so upset, but I've got to tell them . . . *where* is that ambulance?"

Abby had borrowed a jacket from someone to fold and place beneath Sam's head. She racked her brain to think of something comforting to say to Susannah, but all she could think was, Thank God Mattie doesn't have this. This awful thing.

Will, too, wanted desperately to reassure Susannah. He tried, speaking in his customary calm, quiet voice. But he knew she wasn't hearing him.

When the paramedics arrived, he hurried over to them to say grimly, "We've got another fever case here. You'll want masks and gloves on. But let me clear the place first, okay?" He was remembering his mother's firm instructions about not alarming the public. The crowd gathered around Sam shouldn't see the masks and gloves. And hadn't he seen a music reporter from the local paper at a table earlier tonight? Was she still here?

"Well, clear it fast," one of Will's coworkers said abruptly. "Should have been done before we got here."

The rebuke stung, but Will knew the guy was right. He'd been so concerned about Susannah that he hadn't been thinking clearly, or he would have ushered the crowd out of the club immediately after Sam collapsed.

With the help of Abby, the band members, Jeremy, and Kate, Will managed to quickly clear The Music Room. No one wanted to leave, and most of them, Will knew, would hang around out front out of curiosity. But the ambulance had parked out back, so there was a slim possibility that the stretcher could be removed without anyone spotting it.

Will was just beginning to realize how important that was. The sight of paramedics wearing masks was sure to set off a spate of rumors that no explanation from the hospital, no matter how carefully phrased, would defuse.

When the paramedics inserted an IV line into Sam's arm and placed an oxygen mask on his face, Susannah turned so pale, her skin seemed almost translucent. Will ached to comfort her. But she had seen Tina on her stretcher, knew the girl was now in ICU and comatose, had seen the other patients, too. There was nothing he could say to ease her fears.

Zack didn't say anything, either. But he did move closer to Susannah and put a comforting arm around her shoulders as the paramedics lifted the stretcher. She didn't seem to notice.

Will noticed, however, and wished he'd done it first.

Kate, standing beside Will in the now nearly empty club, was astonished by how shocked she was at Sam's collapse. Why did she feel so shaken? He wasn't a close, personal friend of hers. Besides, she was accustomed to illness. Especially lately. So why were her hands shaking, why was her stomach churning so violently, why did she suddenly feel so icy cold?

Because, the answer came, like everyone else in Grant, you saw Samuel Grant III as invincible. Everyone thinks of him as the Golden Boy, the Grant scion and heir who has everything: good looks, good health, piles and piles of money, plenty of friends, a brilliant, safe, secure future without hardship or tragedy. And there he lies on the floor, struck down like any other mortal. As sick as Jenkins Rue, who had nothing.

And if Sam, so protected, so fortunate, could

get this horrible thing, *anyone* could. Anyone at all. Kate thought of her brother Aaron. She thought of her married sister, the husband who loved her, and the little six-year-old boy both of them adored. And she thought of her mother working so closely with the patients in the initial phases of their treatment.

It was bad enough that Damon Lawrence had been brought into the hospital on a stretcher, seriously ill. That had been a real shock. Damon was tall and strong. Like Sam, he'd looked like nothing could hurt him. But it had. And he wasn't any better today, either. She'd checked before she left for the day. A young nurse had told her he'd arrested during the night, but they'd brought him back. "Technically speaking," she had confided in a low voice, "he *died*. But he's hanging in there."

Kate had been thoroughly shaken by the news that Damon had come so close to not making it.

If her family got this horrible thing, too . . .

Her stomach felt hollow.

Susannah rode in the back of the ambulance with Sam, who was conscious and babbling nonsensically. Even when Susannah held one of his hands, he continued to thrash restlessly on the stretcher. The paramedics were in constant touch with ER by radio. Their only instructions had been to make sure Sam had a clear airway and to begin supplying fluids immediately to battle dehydration. The IVs already swung above Sam's head. His vital signs were repeatedly relayed to the hospital.

Will drove Abby and Kate. They sat silently in the front seat, leaning forward slightly in their anxiety, as if that would somehow make the car go faster. Kate knew why Will was rushing to Med Center behind the ambulance. Because of Susannah. He wanted to be there for her. The same went for Abby, because she was Susannah's best friend. What Kate *wasn't* sure of was why *she* was in the car, instead of heading home to Eastridge with her friends.

She'd been so careful not to let herself think of Susannah as a close friend. Not much future in that. Why get to know someone really well when you'll probably never see them again after graduation? Susannah kept insisting she was going to Grant University just like Kate and Abby, but Kate was sure she wasn't being realistic. Susannah's parents would never let her go to Grant. They'd insist on a top Ivy League college for their daughter. The best in the country, probably.

Kate felt a sharp pang of regret. It would have been fun to have Susannah at Grant U. But that would never happen. Which was why she'd guarded so carefully against anything more than a good working relationship with her at ER and an occasional movie or shopping trip to the mall.

But if that had worked the way she intended, then why did she feel like crying, something she hardly ever did, when she thought of how scared Susannah had looked when she climbed into the back of that ambulance? Why was she hurting for Susannah? That hadn't been part of the plan.

In the low-slung, sleek, black sports car directly behind Will's truck, Jeremy drove as fast as he dared, with Callie and Zack urging him on. The tall, glowing buildings of the enormous medical complex loomed directly ahead of them.

Jeremy wondered if his father would be called in to consult on Sam's case. Probably not, unless Sam got so sick his heart became involved.

Zack wondered just how contagious Sam's illness really was.

Callie wondered if her father was in his office, and if Lindsay had come in to work that day, after all.

And Susannah, sitting in the back of the ambulance holding Sam's dry, hot hand, wondered how she was going to tell her parents just how ill their son really was.

chapter
13

The phone call to her parents was the worst Susannah had ever had to make. She waited until Sam had been rushed into a treatment room. There, medical personnel, wearing protective gear as instructed, began pumping him full of cooling fluids and doing the basic groundwork for intensive blood work and specimen cultures. Susannah hated to leave, but her parents had to be notified, and she didn't want someone else doing it.

Nurse Thompson, on night duty, let her use the desk telephone. Susannah's hand was shaking as she punched the number for an outside line, then dialed Linden Hall.

"Oh, hello, dear," her mother said when she recognized Susannah's voice.

"Mother," Susannah interrupted, "I'm at Emsee. Sam is here. He collapsed at The Music Room. We had to call an ambulance. You and Father need to come here right away."

"Sam? Sick? An ambulance?"

"Mother, put Father on the phone, okay?"

"No. No, I'll tell him. We'll be right there. But . . . Sam's not *very* ill, is he, dear? Not like . . . not like Nettie's Tina?" Caroline began speaking very quickly, sudden anxiety forcing words from her mouth on top of one another. "What is it, the flu? Yes, that must be it, Sam has the flu, that's all, you were right this morning, Susannah, I must apologize for not listening. . . ."

"Mother, just come to ER, okay? I'll be waiting for you." Susannah hung up.

Kate, in the treatment room watching Susannah through the glass window, had to admire the way Sam's sister was holding up. No panic there. They were twins, so it wouldn't have been so surprising if Susannah had fallen apart when Sam collapsed. But she hadn't.

In spite of the fact that every single gowned and masked staff member in that room knew exactly who Sam was, she had to admit they hadn't altered their routine one bit. Hadn't called in the Chief of Staff, hadn't taken all personnel off the floors and dragged them into this room, ignoring other emergency cases. Like the man with the metal object imbedded in his left hand, or the baby with croup, or the truck driver stricken by a sudden asthma attack. They were being treated in other rooms. That was one thing Kate liked about Med Center. All patients were treated the same, no matter where they lived or how much money they had. She wasn't sure that was true of all hospitals. But it was true here.

In minutes, plastic bags of intravenous fluids dangled over Sam's head. Throat cultures were taken and blood was siphoned from his arm in hopes of finding a clue to the illness that had felled him. Two of the doctors held a brief argument over the wisdom of doing a spinal tap.

"He's too sick," one said, "and besides, we've done them on the other six. Negative. Every one was negative. Why put him through that if it's not going to tell us anything?"

Susannah stood as close to the table, near Kate and Will, as she was permitted. She didn't like the way Sam looked. Hard to believe that anyone could look worse than Tina when she'd been brought in, but Sam did. The paramedic had taken his temperature in the ambulance. He hadn't announced it, but he'd jotted it down and Susannah had watched the way his fingers looped the zero and then angled a four. One hundred and four degrees! Her heart had lurched sickeningly.

The doctor on call wasn't Izbecki. The woman tending Sam was identified by the name tag on her white jacket as "Margaret Mulgrew, M.D." Susannah had never seen her before. Where was

Dr. Izbecki? He was familiar with these cases. Dr. Mulgrew was wasting precious time asking questions that they already knew had no answers.

"He's got the same thing the others in ICU have," Susannah finally burst out impatiently, startling the team working on her brother. "Take him up there! They'll know what to do. And call Dr. Izbecki. He knows what's going on."

"Wow," Kate breathed from behind her. She nudged Will with her elbow. "I didn't know she had it in her."

"Well, she's right," he said quietly. "We're wasting time here. We can't do anything for Sam down here. He belongs upstairs."

Instead of reprimanding Susannah and sending her from the room in disgrace, Dr. Mulgrew lifted her head and nodded. "The girl is right," she said crisply. "Take him up to ICU. I want all cultures back *yesterday*. If they come back positive for influenza, page me. But," she added heavily, "they won't."

Susannah watched the gurney hurry away, her heart in her throat. The wheels had just disappeared inside the elevator when her parents hurried up the steps outside the wide glass doors. Nervously straightening the collar of her pink smock and smoothing pale tendrils of hair that had escaped her braid, she ran to meet them.

She could tell immediately that her mother

hadn't absorbed the fact of Sam's illness yet, and probably wouldn't until she had actually seen him lying in Isolation hooked up to tubes and wires like a scientific experiment.

Her father seemed more angry than worried. "I just found out," he said tersely as they joined Susannah, "that the Montgomery girl is comatose. Comatose! When did that happen? Why wasn't I told? No one on the Board of Directors was notified. I found out quite accidently when I called Montgomery to ask how soon he thought he could get back to Brazil to finish up that business down there. He told me about his daughter. He also told me that the other cases are every bit as critical." But when he looked at Susannah, she saw anxiety in his eyes. "Your brother doesn't have the same thing, does he?"

She wanted desperately, more than she had ever wanted anything in her life, to say, "No, of course not." She wanted to lie.

She was spared both the truth and a lie when Dr. Mulgrew arrived. "Mr. and Mrs. Grant? Could we sit down over there, please?" she invited, pointing toward the alcove. "You come, too," she said to Susannah. "The patient is your brother, I believe?"

Susannah nodded and moved with them through the corridor.

She glanced once over her shoulder to the quiet corner where a group of people from The Music Room had gathered to await word on Sam's condition. She caught Abby's eyes, shrugged helplessly, then followed her parents and the doctor to the alcove, where she took a seat on a blue padded bench.

When Dr. Mulgrew had finished outlining the harsh truth for the Grants, Caroline sat perfectly still in shocked disbelief, her hands in the lap of her lemon yellow sheath.

Samuel asked exactly what Susannah had expected him to ask. "What are you doing for my son?"

"Everything possible," Dr. Mulgrew answered calmly. "We've closed off our ICU and have moved our other critical patients to other hospitals in the complex. And we've been trying to talk Matthews into calling in outside help, but . . ."

"What kind of help?" Samuel asked sharply.

"Outside virologists. A team, if necessary. Our team here, and it's a good one, hasn't been able to come up with anything except that it's not influenza. Not a known one, anyway. We need people who know more about this stuff than we do. But Matthews is afraid the word will get out. Bad for business, he says."

Susannah's father nodded reluctantly. "He's right. Bad for the lab, too. Grant Pharmaceuti-

139

cals is on the edge of a major breakthrough in medical research. A new herb has been found in the Brazilian rain forest that may pave the way for a cure for several major cancers. An outbreak at Med Center now could seriously jeopardize our research."

Dr. Mulgrew barely hid her disgust. Biting off her words, she said, "We now have *seven* cases of this thing. It is very clearly contagious, and to my mind, if it *is* an influenza, it is not an ordinary one, not a known one, and not easily curable. It can't be treated with aspirin and bed rest and fluids. Antibiotics and antibacterials have been unsuccessful so far." Her steely gaze on Samuel Grant never wavered. "I would like you to pay particular attention to the word *contagious*, please."

Caroline stood up, smoothing her skirt nervously. "All I care about," she said clearly, "is my son. He *is* going to be all right, isn't he? I want to see him." Her voice sank then, and she murmured, "It's my fault. I should have . . ."

"Never mind that now," her husband interjected sharply. He inquired of the doctor, "May I assume that my son is getting the best treatment possible?"

Dr. Mulgrew shrugged. "I can't very well tell you that, can I, Mr. Grant, when I don't even know the nature or origin of the illness yet. Your concern for your son is understandable, but may

I respectfully suggest that you take it upstairs to Matthews? We don't even know what we're looking for here." That said, she turned and hurried away.

Susannah's father turned to her, his eyes accusing. "You *knew* about all of this. You knew Tina was comatose, you knew this thing was contagious . . ."

"And I tried to tell you, didn't I? At least, I tried to tell you that Sam was sick. But you weren't listening, as usual." He was being grossly unfair, but she didn't want to fight with him now. All she cared about was Sam. "I think Dr. Mulgrew's right. You have to talk Mr. Matthews into calling in specialists."

For once, he looked as if he were actually listening. But his expression quickly turned to doubt. "I have to agree with Matthews on one point. If a team of medical investigators comes trooping into Grant, the press will find out. It will be all over the papers that we've got some unknown, contagious disease here."

"Why can't you just tell the press that they're here for a conference or something? Medical people come here from all over the world all the time for meetings and conferences and seminars."

His eyebrows arched. "You're suggesting that we lie?"

Susannah stood up, glancing into the hallway

to find Will's eyes on her. She knew how *he* would answer her father. So she did it for him. "That's a better lie than pretending there's nothing wrong here when there is. It's a safer lie. You say your new drug could save lives. That's great. But what about the lives here, now, up in ICU? Don't they count for anything? One of them is your son, Dad."

She hadn't actually been thinking in terms of death, of course. No one had died. She was just being dramatic to make a point, she told herself. Then she saw Sam's face as he lay on the gurney, and wondered just how far off the mark her statement was.

"Samuel," Caroline said quietly but more firmly than Susannah had ever heard her speak, "if you don't do everything within your power to see to it that our son gets the help he needs, I will never forgive you. Never."

Her husband nodded. "I'll go see Matthews right now. You go on up to ICU. I'll meet you there shortly."

"You might not be allowed to see Sam," Susannah was forced to tell her parents as they all moved upward in the elevator. "He'll be quarantined. You can look at him through the door window, but I don't think they'll let you in. Unless you wear protective gear, and I don't know if they'll okay that."

"They'll let us in," Samuel said confidently.

Susannah supposed they would. He was, after all, Samuel Grant II.

Downstairs, Kate joined Will, standing with Callie, Jeremy, and Zack near the watercooler. Callie made some inane remark about absolutely adoring the purple turtleneck Kate was wearing, which Kate ignored. "I only have a sec," she said quickly. "Things have been piling up, so I decided to lend a hand. We've got a boating accident victim in Two, a nasty case of the croup in Five, and a hand that's lucky to still be attached to an arm in Three." She had barely finished speaking when the wail of an ambulance died directly outside. Although he wasn't on duty, Will ran to help.

To Jeremy, Callie, and Zack, Kate said abruptly, "You might as well go home. Susannah probably won't come back down for a while. And all I can tell you about Sam is that he's got a fever and he's being taken care of. The flu, maybe. You can call ICU later if you want. Maybe they can tell you something." But she knew that wasn't true. How could anyone tell them anything when no one *knew* anything?

Will rushed past them then with a gurney flanked by two paramedics. Callie sucked in her breath, fearful of another case of illness whose germs might be floating around in the air. She tugged on Jeremy's arm. "C'mon, let's get out of here. I need air."

"Caucasian male, forties, unconscious, second- and third-degree burns to portions of his upper torso, arms, neck, and face," they heard then, but Callie didn't stop walking. She heard the words, "Car wreck, trapped inside, gasoline spilled, caught fire," but still she kept going. There was far too much sickness in this place, germs everywhere, even if the new patient didn't have the fever. Since she wasn't allowed to see Tina or Sam, why hang around?

Outside, on the steps, a tall, heavyset, blonde woman walked up to Callie and Jeremy. Callie had the feeling she'd been lying in wait for them. Without introducing herself, the woman asked, "You were at The Music Room tonight, am I right?"

Callie nodded, but Jeremy looked at the woman suspiciously and asked, "Who are you?"

A small white card was extended toward them. They didn't take it. "Sheila Dane, music critic for the *Grant Gazette*. I was at the club, too. I saw what happened. I was wondering what you could tell me about your friend. The one who was taken away in the ambulance."

Jeremy tugged on Callie's arm. "C'mon," he urged, "let's go." To the woman, he said politely, "You'll have to talk to someone inside about that."

"But you were with him. And we've been hearing rumors at the paper that there's some kind of sickness going around. Is that true? Is that what your friend has? What kind of sickness is it?"

Zack came out just then. He paused before passing the trio. "I know you," he said to the woman. "You're the music critic from the paper. So what do we get, a thumbs-up or thumbs-down?"

"To tell you the truth," she said apologetically, "I'd just arrived when that boy collapsed, so I haven't really had a chance to hear you yet. Maybe tomorrow night. That is," she added slyly, with a coy smile, "if you can talk your friends here into giving me the dope on that boy who's sick."

Zack laughed. "Oh, I get it. We tell you what we know, and the band gets a good review? Okay. Never underestimate the power of the press, I always say. So here's what I know about the kid who got sick tonight: nothing." He smiled at the woman. "Now we get a good review, right? Wasn't that the deal?" Laughing again, he ran lightly down the steps and hailed a cab waiting at the curb.

Jeremy began to walk down the steps, too, but Callie stayed where she was, looking at the woman with interest. "You're the press?" She was thinking of the conversation she'd overheard outside her father's office. And she was seeing him again in the arms of his secretary, whom he hadn't fired, after all. And she was thinking, very rapidly, as if her brain had suddenly gone on double time, that if the people in Grant found out that the hospital had been keeping secret news of a terrible, contagious disease, they'd be furious. Then Med Center would be in trouble and so would her father, because he ran the place. He might even lose his job. No problem. Her father was very, very smart and capable. He could get a job anywhere. Lots of people would want to hire him. Maybe he'd get a job where he had lots of time off. A nicer job, where he didn't have to hide important information from people just because of money. Maybe a job with an old, ugly secretary.

"Callie!" Jeremy insisted, reaching out to tug on her arm.

"Jeremy, be careful, you'll tear my new dress." Then, she said sweetly, "You run along now. This nice lady will take me home."

Jeremy took a hesitant step backward. "Callie, what are you doing?"

"Go *on*, Jeremy." Callie waved him away. "See you later."

Jeremy had known Callie a long time. He hesitated another moment or two, then sighed in defeat, turned, and loped on down the steps, turning only once to direct a disapproving glance in her direction.

When he was gone, Callie extended one hand toward the woman and said, "My name is Callie Matthews. My father runs this place. Now, what exactly did you want to know?"

─╮╭─╮╭╮╭─╮╭─╮╭╮╭─

"I don't know how you stand it, working here," Abby said to Susannah the following morning. They were in the hospital's basement cafeteria with Jeremy and Will, sitting at a long, narrow table in a dim corner. The only other people in the stark, white-walled room were residents with weary faces, a few orderlies, and several worried-looking relatives of patients. Conversation had to battle the constant sound of the PA system summoning staff members or announcing a new emergency. Every few minutes, someone in white or surgical green would get up and hurry from the room. The smell of alcohol and antiseptic lingered, overpowering the rich, more pleasant aroma of fresh coffee.

Susannah had spent the night up on the eighth floor, trying to sleep on a sticky, fake-leather couch in the nurses' lounge. Lavender half-moons had appeared under her eyes, and her face was tense with anxiety over Sam. Abby had brought her a change of clothing. She had slipped into the clean white trousers and a peach knit top in the nurses' lounge, not bothering with her smock. She leaned back against the plastic chair, sipping hot coffee. Her pale, wavy hair, which she had brushed thoroughly and left hanging loose, draped itself over the back of the chair, as Abby added, "It's so hectic here, so noisy. And so gruesome. There are so many nicer places to work at Emsee. We don't get any critical-care patients at Rehab. No blood or broken bones or convulsions from fever. That's what makes it nicer."

Susannah, lost in worry over Sam, shrugged absentmindedly. "I like it here," was all she said.

"Callie talked to a reporter last night," Jeremy announced suddenly.

The remark snapped Susannah to attention. But it was Will who cried, "Say that again?"

Jeremy's handsome face flushed an uneasy red. "I said, Callie talked to the music critic from the *Gazette* last night. I haven't seen this morning's paper, so I don't know if they printed anything." He shook his head. "I tried to talk her out of it, but she wouldn't listen."

"A music critic isn't really a reporter." Abby glanced around the table for confirmation. No one nodded in agreement. But Abby persisted. "She doesn't get to write news, does she? All she writes is music reviews."

"Even if that's true," Will said darkly, "she could tell someone else. Her editor, for instance.

He'd never sit on a story like this one. It could be all over the front page this morning." He jumped to his feet. "I'm going to go dig up a paper. Be right back."

"Why would Callie do something like that?" Abby ran a hand through her dark, curly hair. "I can't believe she didn't know better."

Jeremy laughed, a brittle, humorless sound. "Oh, she knew better. Last night when we were following the ambulance here, I told her my dad warned me to keep quiet about the fever, and Callie said, 'Yeah, mine too.' She sounded mad when she said it, though." Jeremy's thick, light-colored brows drew together in a puzzled frown. "I saw the look on her face when she made up her mind to talk to that woman. No way was she innocent. She was doing it deliberately. What I can't figure is why."

"Because she's mean and thoughtless and self-ish, that's why," Abby said firmly.

Jeremy shook his head. "That's not it. I know Callie is spoiled and selfish. My mother always called her 'Bertha Brat.'" His face darkened when he mentioned his mother. "But then, my mother didn't like very many people in Grant. The thing is, Callie doesn't do anything without a reason. Trust me, she's got a reason for talking to that newspaper woman. I just don't know what it is."

"If the *Gazette* prints what's going on here,"

Susannah said, pushing her chair back and standing up, "the phones in every hospital in this complex will be ringing off the hook. We've got every kind of patient there is, people from all over the world. Cardiac patients. Cancer patients. Burn patients. Victims of horrible accidents. Chronically ill people who can't find the right treatment anywhere else. Med Center is the only hope for a lot of these people. If the word gets out that we have something contagious here, relatives of those patients will pull them out of here. Where will those patients go?" Susannah shook her head. "I can't think about that now. All I can think about is Sam. Maybe if it does come out in the paper, my father and the Board will be forced to call in outside help. I still haven't heard if he and Matthews agreed to do that last night. I haven't seen my parents this morning."

"Doesn't anyone know what it is yet?" Jeremy asked. "What they've got? How sick they really are?"

"No."

Jeremy felt a sharp stab of anger. He had come to the hospital first thing this morning to find out how Tina and Sam were, and no one would tell him. Maybe Callie had done them all a favor. Maybe the only way to find out anything was to go to the press, tell the story, and force the hospital to tell them something.

"Is Kate here?" Susannah asked Abby. "I haven't seen her."

"She's upstairs already. Said she wanted to see how the ICU patients were doing. Are you going up there now?"

Susannah nodded. "I want to talk to my father. Maybe now that he's seen how sick Sam and the others are, he's realized we need help here. Outside help."

Telling her friends she'd see them later, she left the cafeteria.

Upstairs in ICU, one of the alarms at the nurses' desk went off.

The two nurses sitting at the station got up and ran, summoning other nurses from other rooms as they went.

So there was no one at the desk when Kate stepped out of the elevator. And no one in the wide hallway. She decided to wander on her own until she found a nurse. There seemed to be some sort of commotion going on in one of the small rooms fronting the hallway. She hadn't heard a "Code Blue," the signal that meant a patient was in serious trouble and all personnel must respond. But the code could have sounded before she arrived on the floor. She ignored that room and moved along the wide corridor to peer in the door windows of other rooms. Every door bore a large placard reading ISOLATION. DO NOT ENTER.

Jenkins Rue, his head turned away from Kate, his injured leg held in traction, lay very still, his eyes closed. Several IVs were running steadily, their needles taped into one arm and the top of a hand, the containers suspended above his head like makeshift mobiles. His chest was bare and dotted with round, white EKG monitors hooked up to a machine beside his bed. She had heard that his CAT scan had revealed no serious head injury. That was good news. Still, the sight of him reminded Kate of the broken toys she used to "doctor" when she was little, lining them up on the back porch and ministering to them with an inexpensive doctor's kit her grandmother had given her.

There was no nurse in the room, which Kate found odd. Weren't all ICU patients supposed to have twenty-four-hour supervision? Maybe that didn't apply when Isolation was involved. Maybe in contagious cases, they were watched mostly by monitors from the nurses' station. But there was no one at the nurses' station. Weird.

In another room, Damon Lawrence lay among a sea of white. Not only did he have electrodes attached to his chest, he also had a breathing tube taped to his face, the tube attached to a ventilator. It was a shocking sight.

Feeling increasingly uneasy, Kate moved slowly along the corridor. The third room contained the middle-aged cleaning-crew foreman, who was hooked up to the same multitude of wires and tubing as the others. But while the others had been lying still, he seemed to be moving restlessly. Did that mean he was getting better? Or worse?

Kate was about to move along the hallway in search of Sam, when a young nurse, masked, capped, and gowned, burst out of a doorway, raced down the hall to the desk, and snatched up the telephone. Kate couldn't hear what she said, but the call only lasted a second. Then the young nurse flew back down the hall to disappear into the same room.

Curious, Kate moved forward, toward that room. She didn't want to interfere. A mere volunteer would never be allowed to help with an intensive care case. The best thing she could do for the patient in that room was stay out of the way.

But then it occurred to her that the patient might be Sam. If something was going terribly wrong in that room, she had to know.

She took a few more steps and found herself standing directly in front of the door. It was closed, but the voices of the half dozen or so nurses and doctors working on the patient were loud, commanding, and she was able to make out some of what they were saying. Shouting, actually. She couldn't see who the patient was, and there was no chart hanging on the wall outside the room. It could be Sam. Or it could be Tina, or the Rollerblading accident victim.

Her own heart began pounding in her chest as she heard someone shout, "The patient is ventilating, damn it!" Then, "Don't you dare die on me, you hear me?"

Kate's blood chilled. Die? She pressed her face up against the glass, straining to hear, trying to see beyond the furiously active medical staff blocking her view of the patient. They were all bent over the bed. She saw paddles, saw a nurse applying gel, saw her hand the paddles to a tall figure in white, saw the paddles descend, saw feet jerk.

Kate pulled back to glance again at the sign on the door. There it was, ISOLATION. DO NOT ENTER. According to that sign, the patient in this room suffered from the mysterious flu of unknown origin. Not heart disease.

But there in front of her was the crash cart, there were the paddles, set aside for the moment while someone in a blue coverall worked strenuously at closed-chest heart massage.

It must not have worked, because the paddles were handed over again. When they had been slapped down upon the chest, the feet sticking out from beneath the sheet jerked once again. Kate knew that wasn't necessarily a sign of life. Just a reflex from the electrical current.

She waited, holding her breath, straining to

see the monitor beside the bed. But it was turned slightly away from her, and she couldn't tell if the line was flat.

"What's up?" a voice asked in her ear.

Kate gasped and jumped.

"Sorry," Susannah said quietly, peering into the door window. "Didn't mean to scare you. What's going on?"

Kate still didn't know who the patient was. It could be Sam. "I . . . I'm not sure. I guess someone's in trouble."

"Who?"

"I don't know."

Susannah glanced around the hallway. "Are my parents up here?"

"Haven't seen them. Maybe they went downstairs for coffee."

"That isn't Sam in there, is it? Kate?"

"I don't know," Kate said again.

Then they both heard, as clearly as if they'd been standing in the room, an emotionless voice stating, "No pulse."

And both shuddered as a long, wicked-looking needle appeared, poised to plunge directly into the heart. If that didn't work . . .

It didn't.

"Clear!" they heard, and the paddles smacked down again. This time, the lurching motion was more violent.

Because of the masks and caps, Kate and Susannah could see no facial expressions on any of the medical staff. But they could tell from the body language that their attempts at reviving the patient were fruitless.

They tried valiantly for another very long five minutes. Kate had stayed calm up until the very last minute or two. She stayed calm because she fully expected success. She had been lucky so far in her volunteer work. No one had died in ER while she was on duty. Even patients who had suffered full cardiac arrest had been resuscitated every single time. She expected that to happen this time, too, right up until the last minute or two.

"Who do you think it is?" Susannah asked breathlessly. Her face, too, was pressed up against the glass. She was trembling, and her face was chalky.

"It's not Sam, Susannah. I'm sure it isn't." Kate wasn't sure of any such thing, but it killed her to see Susannah so scared.

They had every intention of remaining in front of the door until they knew who was in that bed. But a nurse looked up, saw them, and angrily waved them away.

They left reluctantly, but they didn't go very far. If they waited in the hall long enough, someone would have to tell them something.

Leaning against the wall opposite the room where the frenzied activity was taking place, they talked quietly to hide their anxiety. Susannah told Kate about Callie's interview with the newspaper woman.

Kate's response was, "What could Callie talk to her about? Callie doesn't know anything. She doesn't work here. Wouldn't be caught dead working here. There's no way she could know how sick Tina really is. So what could she have told the woman?"

"Maybe her father told her that Tina's comatose."

"He wouldn't have. He'd be too worried that she'd tell everyone. He's her father, he must know what a big mouth she has."

They stopped talking when a nurse came out of the room and sank into a wooden, straight-backed chair against one wall. When she reached up and pulled off her mask, they saw that she was young. Her face was as white as the stacks of clean linens they often carried from one cubicle to another in ER. And they saw that she was crying. Quietly. Not even bothering to wipe the tears away. They dripped down her cheeks and onto the blue coverall she was wearing over her uniform.

Kate and Susannah exchanged a glance of dread. The nurse had left the door to the room slightly ajar. The sounds coming from inside had changed. The shouting had ended. Footsteps had stopped rushing from bed to machine to supply cabinet. They moved slowly now, heavily. The earlier sharp, staccato commands had been replaced by a dull murmur of voices.

The crisis was over.

Slowly, Kate and Susannah moved to stand next to the nurse's chair. Susannah, her eyes dark blue with fear, was the first to speak. "What's wrong?" She glanced at the plastic name tag on the coverall. "Nurse Fielding? What's happened?"

Mary Fielding lifted her head. "I know I'm supposed to be objective," she said, her voice choked with tears. "But I can't help how I feel. That girl was only seventeen years old. Just two years younger than me."

Kate saw the undisguised relief in Susannah's face at the word "girl." The patient wasn't Sam. There were two girls in ICU. Tina Montgomery, and the victim of the Rollerblading accident. When that thought registered, something else registered as well, and the relief in Susannah's eyes was instantly replaced by new anxiety.

Because the nurse had used the word "was." She hadn't said, "That girl is only seventeen years old." She had said, "That girl was only seventeen years old."

"Which girl?" Kate asked hoarsely.

"That Montgomery girl. She was so young!"

"Was?" Susannah breathed.

Mary Fielding regarded them with moist blue eyes. "That girl died," she answered slowly, as if she wasn't quite ready to believe it herself yet. "They tried everything. They really did. But she died a few minutes ago."

chapter
15

Lost in shock, Kate and Susannah didn't hear the elevator arriving at the eighth floor. When Abby suddenly appeared in front of them waving a newspaper, they stared at her blankly.

"There is an article in the paper . . ." she began, but broke off to say, "Hey, you guys look like you just lost your best friend." Then she noticed the nurse, who was still crying quietly. "Uh-oh, what's going on?" Round, dark eyes moved to Susannah's face. "It's not Sam, is it?"

"No," Kate said then, standing up straighter, her eyes losing the blank look of shock.

Susannah's eyes met Abby's. She cleared her throat. "Tina Montgomery just died."

Abby gasped. "Died? Tina? Are you sure?"

The young nurse wiped her eyes and got to her feet. "I've got to get back in there." To Abby, she said, "Like I told your friends here, we tried everything to keep that girl alive. She was just too sick."

"With what?" Kate asked quickly. "Do they know?"

The question caught Mary Fielding off guard. "Oh." She thought for a minute, her lips pursed. "No, I don't think they do." Slowly, reluctantly, as if she were going to her own doom, she walked back to Tina's room and disappeared inside.

"I want to see Sam!" Susannah said urgently. "I need to see my brother, *now*!"

Nodding, Kate moved swiftly to a cart beside the nurses station. She flipped quickly through the medical charts until she found the one she wanted. When her eyes had scanned it, she announced, "Room F. Sam's in Room F." She dropped the chart back into place and the three girls moved down the hall to a room with a large red *F* over the doorway.

They couldn't see much through the door window. Sam was there, attached to the usual network of wires and snaking tubing, but his head was turned away from the door, his body covered to the waist. They could, however, see that his chest was rising and falling evenly, which was all Susannah cared about. Sam might be very, very sick, but he was still alive. Unlike Tina Montgomery.

They had just turned away from the door when Susannah's parents stepped out of an elevator. When they saw the trio gathered in front of Sam's room, Caroline hurried her steps. "Susannah, what's wrong?" she cried when she was still some distance away.

Susannah waited to answer until they were close enough to allow her to speak quietly. When she had told them about Tina, Caroline's eyes filled with tears.

Samuel's reaction was one of anger. "Damn! Last night I let Matthews talk me into holding off on a call to outside experts. His arguments made sense: We have good people here, there have only been seven cases, there'd be no way to keep it quiet, the resulting publicity would be bad for the entire complex, and no one had died . . . and now this!"

"If this . . . this *thing* can kill," his wife said heatedly, "you have no business keeping it quiet. People should be told! They should be *warned*!"

"They know now," Abby said, holding up the newspaper in her hand. "There's an article in this morning's *Gazette*. Front page."

"Let me see that!" Susannah's father reached for the paper.

"Everyone's going to find out now, anyway," Kate pointed out coldly. "Even Matthews can't keep Tina's obituary out of the newspaper, right?"

Samuel winced. But he said as his eyes scanned the newspaper article, "All they will learn from that is that a seventeen-year-old girl is dead. They won't learn what she died of, because no one seems to know. But," he added as he handed the newspaper back to Abby, "we're going to find out. Caroline, you stay here with Sam. I'm going to see Matthews and I'm not leaving that office until he's made a call for outside help."

Susannah stayed with her mother, who was visibly shaken by the news of Tina's death.

Kate and Abby went back downstairs. In the elevator, Abby said, "Well, it's awful about Tina, but at least Mr. Grant is going to find out what this horrible thing is."

An unforgiving Kate said, "Yeah. Too bad he didn't do it before someone died."

"Kate!"

"Well, it's true, isn't it? I wasn't a member of Tina Montgomery's fan club, and I guess you weren't either. But she didn't deserve to die, did she? If they'd brought outside help in faster, maybe she'd still be alive. And do you really think Samuel Grant II would be moving his butt now if his own son weren't sick? I don't think so."

Abby didn't like to hear Med Center criticized. "He probably thought the people here could figure it out, Kate. The best research people in the country are here. Who knew how bad this thing could get?"

"If they're the best people in the country," Kate responded tartly as the elevator doors slid open, "why didn't they know it would get this bad?"

"Because it's something new," Abby persisted.

"Something different. That's why none of the tests they did showed anything. And I don't know about you, Kate, but I'm scared. What if Matthews agrees to call in outside help and they can't figure out what it is? How many more people are going to die like Tina before someone comes up with an answer?"

"Maybe none," Kate said, changing her tactics. No point in arguing with Abby about Med Center. She had the same blind spot as Susannah. Yes, Med Center was wonderful, yes, some brilliant work was being done here, and no, there wasn't any place else in the world where Kate would feel safer if she fell ill. But that didn't mean it was perfect. "Maybe it was one of those bugs that attack really fast and then disappear. No one ever knows where they come from or what caused them. We've read about them, remember?"

An ambulance's wail outside forced Abby to raise her voice slightly. "I remember. But the diseases I read about came from rain forests and jungles, Kate. The last time I looked, Grant didn't have a rain forest or a jungle."

"People travel, Abby. And sometimes when they leave the country, they come back with more than presents for their relatives. Anyway," Kate added as they separated in the hall, "let's just hope Sam's was the last case."

And for a few peaceful days, it looked that

way. There were no new cases. The prominent virologist Dr. John Beck, whom Matthews had finally agreed to summon, flew in from Germany and settled in a large but airless, fully-equipped room at Grant Pharmaceuticals to study all of the cultures and specimens sent over. The news of his arrival somewhat placated the people of Grant, inflamed by Callie's newspaper interview. The truth had been kept from them, and that made them angry. But something was being done now. They would hold off on action against the medical complex until this doctor with all the initials after his name gave them some answers.

Tina's funeral was held on a Tuesday marred by a thick, humid fog that coated the mourners, the hearse, and the green canvas canopy with a damp, glistening film. Susannah and her mother wept for Tina and for Tina's parents, who had lost their only child.

The other six patients held their own, not getting better, but becoming no worse. Only Damon Lawrence required the aid of a machine to help him breathe.

Dr. Beck insisted that all medical personnel be retested, also all of the relatives of the seven patients to date. The wait to hear the results was excruciating, and tempers flared more than once in ER. The strain was showing.

When the residents of Grant heard about the

testing, they showed up in hordes at ER, demanding to be tested as well. Eventually, the lab at Grant Pharmaceuticals took over that job, testing anyone who insisted upon it.

All of the results were negative.

"It is absolutely viral, not bacterial," the virologist, a short, white-haired man, told Samuel Grant at the dinner table in Linden Hall on Friday night. "A fever of unknown origin. I must tell you that my fear is, it could be one we haven't seen before. That would not be good. However, it is clearly not a hemorrhagic fever. You may be grateful for that, Mr. Grant. That is a blessing, I promise you."

"So, what do we do?"

"There is more testing to be done. Then if what I suspect is true, you will need to contact your Centers for Disease Control. In the state of Georgia, is it not?"

Samuel bristled. "We were hoping to avoid that, Dr. Beck. This is why we contacted you instead of calling the CDC. We want some answers here, but we would like to avoid the publicity associated with bringing in their field people. The word always gets out, no matter how careful you are. Bad public relations. What can the people in Atlanta do that you can't?"

"Many things. I am a researcher of disease, Herr Grant. That is what I do. But if what I suspect is true, we will need to find someone who was infected with the illness but fought it successfully. Perhaps he or she became mildly symptomatic, but quickly recovered. Or never became ill at all, which would, of course, make our search that much more difficult, since that patient would not even be aware that he had *been* ill. Might have believed that he had a touch of the flu. If we *could* find him, however, we could use the antibodies in that person's blood to come up with a vaccine. We could do that quickly, with the marvelous equipment you have in your laboratory. But first the person must be located, and that I cannot do for you. Your CDC will be better able to help you there."

Susannah didn't see how they could find that person when they had no idea *where* the illness had originated. Many people in Grant traveled internationally. The task of poring over every airline manifest for the past month or longer seemed to her overwhelming, even with the help of computers. Some people took ships across the ocean because they feared or disliked flying. Those people would have to be considered, too.

"Tina's father traveled," she volunteered as Marcella served chocolate mousse. "Remember, Father? You said he was checking out a new drug. In South America?"

Her father nodded. "I've already talked to him. He stayed in a five-star hotel in Brazil, never left the room except to go to meetings, and even those were held in the hotel. He didn't go wandering around any jungles or rain forests. He was so busy he even took most of his meals in his hotel. And other than becoming airsick, which is normal for him, he wasn't sick. So . . ."

"Still," Dr. Beck said, "I would like to talk to this man. Could you perhaps set up such a meeting?"

Samuel shook his head. "That would be difficult just now. It was his daughter who died. He's taking it hard. I've given him some time off and the key to our cabin in the Berkshires. He and his wife have, I believe, already left town. There is no telephone up there. We go for peace and quiet." He settled back in his chair and lifted his coffee cup. "Isn't it a good sign that there have been no new cases these past few days?"

The doctor shrugged. "Perhaps. But as you do not yet have an epidemic here, it becomes clear that this particular disease is not easily spread. Or perhaps many people have an inborn immunity to it. There may be others who, while not immune, are able to resist it for longer periods of time than those who have already fallen ill. I was told, for example, that the girl who died had had an influenza a short while ago. That would have weakened her immune system. I was also told in answer to my questions that the boy on the ventilator kept late hours and took very poor care of his health. Your own son, I believe," he said, waving his spoon toward Samuel, "was extremely active and might have been fatigued."

Susannah saw her father's lips tighten. He didn't like the suggestion that Sam was actually capable of becoming overtired. How silly. Sam was human, wasn't he? Anyone on his hectic social schedule would become tired. Some people might even admit it.

"In each of those cases," the doctor continued, "the immune system could have been functioning poorly, making them easy targets for our fever. You could have people in your community who actually have the disease now, but are resisting it better because they take excellent care of themselves. They might think they have a summer 'bug,' as you call it, or believe they are simply overtired or suffering from allergies. Unless they have an inborn immunity, they will eventually show up at your hospital. In other words, the fever could still be spreading. Quietly. Taking its time. Another reason why I would suggest you call your CDC in Georgia."

Susannah's heart sank. They might have more cases in town, even now?

Caroline had been listening quietly to the doctor's words. Now, she said to Susannah, "Perhaps we should think about canceling the fashion show. If what Dr. Beck says is true . . . and I'm sure it is," she added hastily, sending a quick smile the doctor's way, "gathering so many people together at one time in one place would be foolish. If we have no way of knowing who is sick and who isn't. I would hate to be responsible for . . ."

"We are not canceling any events scheduled for Med Center!" her husband interrupted, slamming his hand down on the lace tablecloth. When they all stared at him, he lowered his voice to add more calmly, "We will let Dr. Beck finish his tests. If he doesn't come up with anything, I'll talk to Matthews about contacting the CDC. But for right now, life goes on as usual, is that clear?"

Susannah regarded him with incredulity. "But it *isn't*!" She carefully folded her white linen napkin and placed it beside her plate, her dinner only half eaten. "How can you say that? Life *isn't* going on as usual! Look around this table, Father. Do you see Sam sitting here anywhere? You don't, because he's not here! He's lying in a hospital bed in Intensive Care at Emsee." She stood up, left her chair, pushed it back into place. "So please don't talk about life going on as usual." She turned to her mother. "Yes," she said clearly, "I think you *should* cancel the fashion show. And I think if the people in this town knew the whole truth about this horrible disease, they wouldn't step one foot outside their houses until someone comes up with some answers. May I be excused? I want to go see Sam."

Caroline nodded. Susannah told the doctor politely that it had been nice meeting him, and without saying a word to her father, left the room.

Five minutes later, at 8:10 P.M. at a pool party held not far from the foot of Linden Hill, two members of the Grant High School football team advanced upon seventeen-year-old Sally Kent, who was lying listlessly on a chaise lounge in her pink bikini, holding a wet paper towel to her forehead. It was clear to the crowd around the pool that the boys had every intention of tossing pretty, popular Sally into the deep blue water.

"Leave me alone!" she warned as they continued to advance. "I don't want to swim! I don't feel good. My head is splitting. Go away!"

"Nope," the larger of the two boys said, grinning. "This is a *pool* party, Sally, and you haven't gone near the water. We can't have that. C'mon, be a sport."

Sally Kent had never felt so sick in her life. And that scared her, because a girl she hardly knew, a girl who supposedly had been a very healthy athlete, just like herself, had *died* after being in the hospital just a few days. She knew she should be in bed. She knew she shouldn't have come to this stupid party. But she had hoped it would make her feel better. Only it hadn't. She felt worse. Much worse.

"I am *not* going in that water!" she insisted as the boys reached her. They ignored her. One picked up her legs, the other her arms, and as she screamed a protest, they began swinging her.

"Hey, guys," the hostess, a girl named Pinky Dwyer, shouted from the open glass patio door, "you gotta see this! Bill Conti is actually swinging from the dining room chandelier! Come see!"

Laughing, everyone but the two football players and Sally Kent jumped up and ran into the house.

"I gotta see that," the larger of the two boys said. "Let's dump her." They tossed a still-screaming Sally out into the middle of the pool. She landed with a splash and sank immediately.

Then, laughing, the two boys ran into the house to watch their teammate make a total fool of himself. They knew Sally Kent was an excellent swimmer. So they didn't wait to make sure she came back up to the surface.

She didn't.

chapter
16

Will didn't mind working nights. The night ambulance runs were usually more interesting.

The call came into the hospital shortly after eight-thirty from a 911 operator at the police station. "Respond to a possible drowning, 11856 Arrowroot Drive, intersection Arrowroot and Linden Hill Boulevard, facing north. Victim young female. See homeowner name of Dwyer."

Will's heart jumped. Linden Hill? Susannah's road. But the address wasn't on Linden Hill, he told himself as he climbed into the ambulance. The young female victim was at a house below the hill, just off the boulevard. Could be someone Susannah knew, but it couldn't be her, he thought as the siren came on and the vehicle raced from the garage, out of the complex, and north on Grant Avenue.

Susannah came around the final curve at the foot of Linden Hill, prepared to increase her speed as she hit the long, straight, tree-lined boulevard. She was anxious to get to Emsee and find out how Sam was doing. But what she saw ahead of her as she braked for the stop sign kept her feet from moving to the accelerator.

Cars lined Arrowroot on both sides of the street, which spelled "party" to Susannah. Nothing unusual there. The corner house facing Susannah was Pinky Dwyer's house. Pinky had a lot of parties. But there were also two police cars and a fire truck in front of the house, a large split-level, brightly lit. No smoke or flames were visible, but it occurred to Susannah as she hesitated at the stop sign that what looked like bright lights inside the house could actually be flames. A fire?

Pinky Dwyer wasn't a close friend of Susannah's. Susannah knew she was popular at Grant High. Thus the parties. Sometimes they were pretty wild, or so she'd heard. She'd never been invited to one. If someone had accidentally set the house on fire, this party must have been even wilder than usual.

Susannah set the Benz in motion. Her intention was to drive by. Whatever the emergency, it was being handled by police and firemen and she'd only be in the way. A siren and the red roof light of an ambulance approaching from the other direction changed her mind. Maybe she could be of some help. Deciding quickly, she pulled the Benz over to the curb and parked behind the two police cars.

When she left the car, she could see immediately that there was no fire in or around the house. Excited voices from the rear of the house carried easily through the quiet evening. Whatever the emergency, it was going on back there, behind the high privacy fence.

Susannah waited on the curb for the paramedics. If they couldn't use her, she would leave, get out of their hair. After she found out what was going on back there.

The ambulance screeched to a halt and Will jumped from the back, along with his partner and, a moment later, the driver. Will was carrying a resuscitator and a cardiac monitor, his partner toted the radio and drug box.

"What's going on?" Susannah asked as they began to run toward the back gate. "Can I come?"

He nodded. "Possible drowning."

Of course. Pinky liked to boast about the pool. "Is it Pinky?"

"Don't know yet. Come on. You can help."

Susannah felt a rush of warmth for Will. She was given so few chances to be of help at the hospital. Maybe she could actually do some good here.

As they yanked the back gate open, she said quickly, "You're not wearing masks, Will."

"It's a drowning, Susannah, not a fever patient."

"You don't know that. Kate's mom said you

guys are supposed to wear masks on all calls until you know for sure that fever isn't involved, remember?"

"You're right." He ran back to the ambulance, returning a minute later to pass out masks. He handed Susannah one, and she put it on, lifting the hair that hung loose around her shoulders.

"Thanks for reminding me," Will said. "Completely forgot."

So she had already helped. It felt good.

The pool area was crowded, a sea of figures in bathing suits, all silent. The only sound was the soft hum of the pool's filter. Moonlight shone on the dark blue water in the pool, empty now except for a lone white rubber float bumping up against the tiled sides.

A limp figure, wet hair splayed out beneath its head, lay on the sea-blue tile on its back while a fireman in uniform administered mouth-to-mouth resuscitation. He stopped just long enough to inform the paramedics that the patient was unconscious and not breathing. Will asked him to continue his resuscitation efforts, using the valve and mask as Will began giving the patient one hundred percent oxygen.

Susannah heard quiet crying in the group forming a semicircle around the victim. Two boys in swimming trunks, boys she recognized as Grant High School football players, were kneeling beside the unconscious girl. Jeremy, in shorts and a sopping-wet T-shirt, sat on the tile directly behind them. All three faces were tense with shock.

"Move the crowd back, Susannah," Will ordered. In a different tone of voice, he announced, "Pulse fifty and weak," then, "sinus bradycardia."

Susannah knew what that meant. It meant the girl lying on the tile, whom she now recognized as Pinky's friend Sally Kent, was in serious trouble. The girl wasn't suddenly going to begin coughing up pool water and sit up, asking what had happened. That pool water had already left her lungs and was circulating throughout her system. She was acidotic, not a good thing. Not good at all.

Using the radio, Will's partner contacted Emsee directly. "Patient unresponsive," he said. "Pupils dilated and reacting sluggishly. Heart rate 68 with ventilation. Blood pressure 108 over 60. No spontaneous respirations."

He turned from the radio to say to Susannah, "Get that crowd back!"

Without hesitation, she began the thankless task of pushing anxious friends of Sally's backward, toward the patio, under strings of brightly colored plastic lights in the shape of fish. Jeremy and the two football players stayed where they were. They weren't in the way, and something about the expressions on their faces kept Susannah from attempting to move them.

The disembodied voice from the hospital, when given complete information on the victim's current condition, ordered an esophogeal airway.

Susannah saw Will hesitate. Tricky business, opening an airway, especially with a patient as small as Sally.

Sure enough, Will's partner, a tall, thin woman Susannah knew as Rita Black, argued with the hospital. But since Sally was still unconscious and not breathing on her own, the voice on the radio insisted.

It was Rita who put the EOA in, not Will. Susannah was almost as relieved as he must have been. Rita had far more experience dealing with esophogeal airways than Will. It was difficult. But with care and a few tense words muttered under her breath, Rita managed the procedure, effectively opening an airway for the patient. She checked Sally's chest to make sure she had been successful, then informed the hospital.

The hospital voice ordered the necessary drugs, which Will inserted in the IV he had already set up.

"Is she dead?" Pinky Dwyer asked Susannah when the crowd had successfully been pushed back against the patio doors. "Is Sally dead?"

"I don't know. What happened?"

Pinky wasn't crying, but her voice was agitated as she tried to explain. "She said she didn't feel very well. She wasn't even going to come tonight.

I talked her into it. She said she had a really bad headache, but I thought she was just mad because Russ Swanson didn't ask her to the party." Pinky took a breath and added nervously, "So you guys don't need those masks, right? I mean, they're pretty creepy. And no one here is sick."

Sally had had a bad headache? Susannah was very glad she'd remembered the masks.

"You still haven't told me what happened." Susannah watched with the others as Sally was loaded onto the gurney, a rolled-up towel beneath her shoulders to help keep the airway open. The fireman continued to ventilate her as they hurried from the pool area, Will and Rita carrying the equipment. Will waved to Susannah, signaling her to come with them.

Pinky looked uncertain. "Well, I guess she just fell in. Jeremy pulled her out. We were all inside, and then Jeremy came back out here. I heard him yelling, and when I got here, he was pulling her out of the pool and yelling at me to call 911. So I did. Jeremy gave her CPR until the firemen arrived. Is Sally going to be all right?"

"Don't know. You guys should all go home. Looks like the party's over. Call her parents, okay? Tell them to come to the ER."

Pinky burst into tears. "Oh, I can't, I can't! They'll blame me! They'll hate me!"

"Pinky," Susannah's voice was stern. "Call

them. Right *now*!" Then she ran to catch up to Will.

"I'm coming, too!" Jeremy called, and followed, his clothes dripping on the grass. Susannah couldn't quite grasp the image of Jeremy as a hero. But he was. He had probably saved Sally Kent's life. If she lived.

"Is she going to be okay?" Susannah asked when the patient had been loaded into the ambulance.

Will's voice was grim. "Don't know. It's too early to tell. She must have been under for more than a few minutes. Where the hell was everyone, that's what I want to know? How could a girl drown at a crowded party?" He climbed inside the vehicle, then turned back to Susannah. "Want to ride along?" He glanced over at the parked Benz. "I can bring you back to your car later."

"Sure. Thanks."

"I'll meet you at the hospital," Jeremy called, and hurried off to his own car.

As Will helped Susannah climb into the back of the ambulance, she said, "I think you should take her temperature."

The driver slammed the doors shut and hurried around to the front.

Overhearing Susannah's suggestion, Rita looked interested. "Temp? Well, we will, but why?"

"Because the girl who held the party said Sally . . . the patient . . . wasn't feeling well when she arrived. I guess if the pool water was cold, that could have lowered her temp, kind of like a refrigerating blanket. But if she did have a fever, wouldn't it be back up by now? Just check, okay?"

Sally Kent's temperature was only 101 degrees.

"But it shouldn't even be that," Rita said. "I think maybe you were right, Susannah. Thanks for reminding us about the masks."

"If she's sick, that fireman was exposed. Jeremy, too. They both gave Sally mouth-to-mouth."

"Well, I don't know about your friend Jeremy, but Tom's fit as a fiddle. It'd take a lot to make him sick. I heard that all of the fever victims were pretty run down before they got it, so I guess Tom's safe enough," Rita said.

Maybe. But could the same be said for all of those party guests at Pinky's? If Sally Kent had the fever, every single one of those guests had been exposed. And from what she'd heard about Pinky's crowd, they kept pretty late hours and their favorite form of exercise was partying. They could be "run down," as Rita had put it.

There had to have been thirty or forty people at that party. If even half of them got sick . . .

At the hospital, Sally was quickly transferred to a hospital gurney and rushed to a trauma room. Dr. Mulgrew spoke briefly with Will and Rita. Then she got busy. She checked Sally's lung sounds and her pupils. Her eyes above the mask seemed to Susannah full of concern as she ordered blood gases, a portable chest X ray, a CBC, and electrolytes. Then, as the orders were being obeyed, she spent a quick few minutes in a second consultation with Rita and Will before returning to her patient.

"What did she say?" Susannah asked as Will joined her in the doorway. "Is Sally going to be okay?"

"Who knows? Dr. Mulgrew's worried about pulmonary edema developing. But that's not Sally's only problem. They weren't going to send her up to ICU because it's all Isolation now, but when we told her about the temp, she checked for other signs of the fever. And found them. So they're sending her upstairs."

Only then did Susannah remember why she had been on her way to the hospital. "I want to see Sam," she said in the same urgent tone of voice she had used when she learned of Tina's death. She looked up at Will with despair in her face. "I thought it was over. That there weren't going to be any more new cases. Didn't you?"

"No." The certainty in his voice surprised her. "I didn't think that. Because we never found the source. Doesn't seem to me that anyone has tried very hard, either. There is probably a carrier out there in Grant somewhere, Susannah, and no one knows who it is. That person will just keep spreading the disease until he or she is found. Thanks to Med Center's aversion to publicity, for which we can all thank Matthews, whoever the person is probably doesn't have a clue that he or she is dangerous."

"But that article in the newspaper . . ."

Will made a sound of disgust as he pushed the elevator button. "That article didn't give one single decent bit of information. It was all hints and innuendo, typical Callie Matthews garbage. And there hasn't been a word printed since, except for that stupid little piece of public relations after Tina died. Blaming her for not getting help sooner."

Susannah fell silent. She didn't want to argue with Will. Besides, she knew he was right. Emsee *should* be doing more to get the word out. Hiring a virologist from another country and hiding him out in a room at the lab wasn't accomplishing what was really necessary . . . which was getting to the origin of the disease. Where was it *coming* from?

"What do you think should be done?" she asked as she pushed the elevator button. "I mean, if you were running things, what would you do?"

His answer was swift and certain. "Call the CDC."

Exactly what Dr. Beck had suggested to her father, Susannah thought with a pang. And her father had refused.

"I'm going to see if I can cheer up Jeremy," Will said, pointing to a chair in the hallway holding a dejected-looking figure. Someone had given Jeremy a white towel. He had draped it around his shoulders, and his head was down. "He saved that girl's life, and no one's paid any attention to him since we got here. Come back down when you're done upstairs and I'll drive you to your car. I'm due for a break, anyway."

Upstairs, the nurse at the desk didn't want to let Susannah into Sam's room. She pointed toward the door. "You see that sign? It says DO NOT ENTER. It's for your own protection, Miss Grant."

"Oh, for heaven's sake!" Susannah cried, "I've already been exposed in ER, before we knew what anyone had. I am *going* in to see my brother. I'll suit up. I'll even wear goggles. But I *am* going in there."

And she did. The nurse gave in. There *were* advantages to being Samuel Grant's daughter.

Feeling strange in the weird protective gear, Susannah sat beside Sam's bed, holding the hand that hadn't been pierced with an IV needle, talking to him in a low, steady voice. He lay perfectly still, his face ashen, his eyes closed, the monitor at his head reflecting a steady zigzagging line that reassured Susannah. As long as that line wasn't flat. . . .

"I know we don't always get along," she said quietly, tears filling her eyes. "And I know we're not like lots of other twins who can read each other's thoughts practically and finish each other's sentences and have the same tastes and habits. I know you're disappointed sometimes because I'm not as much fun as you are. And sometimes I'm disappointed because you don't like the same books and movies that I do." The tears slid from her eyes and down her cheeks. "But I love you like crazy. I love you because you're like the other side of me, the side I'd like to be but can't because that's just not who I am. I always figured that you need the steadier part of me, and I need the fun part of you, and that together we almost make a perfect person. Right?" Susannah reached up with her gloved hand to wipe the tears sliding into her mask. "So you can't die on me. I need you, and you need me. It would be really rotten of you to desert your own twin. So you just hurry up and get better, okay?"

A light tapping on the door window brought Susannah's head up. Her mother was standing in the hall.

"I mean it, Sam." Susannah began to slip her hand from his and, just for a second, thought she had met resistance, thought that his fingers had refused to let go. But when she looked down at him, he was lying perfectly still, his eyes were still closed, and there was no expression on his face.

She pulled her hand free and stood up. Then she went to the door to let her mother take her place.

chapter
17

"Is she dead?" Jeremy asked as Will took a seat beside him. Jeremy's face was white and drawn, his eyes red-rimmed from diving deep into the pool to pull Sally Kent to safety. "Is Sally dead?"

"No. But she would be if it weren't for you, Barlow." Will draped a dry, thick white towel over Jeremy's shoulders. "You're a hero, kid. What I want to know is, where was everybody while that girl was drowning? Why was she out here all alone?"

Jeremy explained about the chandelier stunt. "Tom and Peak feel rotten about throwing her in. She's a good swimmer. Why didn't she come back up?"

"She was too sick. She's got the fever."

Jeremy's head shot up. "I gave her mouth-to-mouth. Before the firemen got there." His face went even paler. "So I guess I'll get it, too, now, right?"

"Not necessarily. Must not be all that easy to get, or the whole town would have it. I know you haven't been sick lately. Do you know if Sally has?"

Some of Jeremy's color returned. "She had a bad head cold a couple of weeks ago. We went to the movies one night, and she coughed the whole time. Very annoying. People kept giving us dirty looks, but she said she couldn't help it. We left before the movie was over."

"Well, that's it, then," Will said, his voice kind. "Her immune system wasn't up to par because of that cold. But you didn't get it, right?"

"No. I haven't had a cold since I was a kid."

"So you're not run down, and you're feeling fine, and I don't think you should worry. Look, Jeremy, you saved a life tonight. That's no small thing. Why don't you just enjoy feeling good about that? Don't make your life miserable by worrying about something that probably isn't going to happen."

There was a commotion at the door, and a rushing of feet toward them. A man and a woman, the woman armed with a microphone, the man with a video camera, joined the pair seated in the hallway. "Which one of you saved that girl's life?" the woman asked.

Will grinned. "Ah, your fifteen minutes of fame are about to begin, Barlow. Enjoy!" He stood up and bowed dramatically in front of the newspeople, then waved a hand in Jeremy's direction. "Here's your hero. Make him look good, okay?"

Instead of being pleased by the sudden attention, Jeremy shrank back against the chair. "Don't leave me here with them!" he begged Will, his voice low. "I don't trust them. Remember Callie's interview?"

"This is not the same thing at all," Will argued, moving away toward the elevator to wait for Susannah. "You deserve this, Barlow. The whole town should know what you did tonight. Relax! And smile nice for the camera."

Susannah stepped out of the elevator then, to find Will waiting for her.

Although her eyes were slightly pink from crying, she smiled when she saw what was happening in the lobby. "I wonder if Dr. Barlow will cut Jeremy's picture out of the paper tomorrow and post it on the hospital bulletin board?"

"Barlow's a busy man. Maybe he doesn't have time to read the paper."

"Well, Jeremy will just have to make sure his father sees the article, that's all. He can tape it to the bathroom mirror or something. Dr. Barlow should know that he's not the only member of that family who saves lives."

Will had already signed out for his break. As they left the building, he said quietly but firmly, "You know your dad has to call in the CDC, don't you? Mulgrew said Sally has the fever, too. That's another new case. So it isn't over."

That really wasn't what Susannah had been expecting or hoping for in the way of conversation. It caught her off guard and she found herself feeling defensive. "It's really not up to my father. Matthews runs the hospital."

They started down the wide, stone steps. A siren close by forced Will to wait with his reply. When it had died down, he laughed and said, "Come on, Susannah! Matthews may run the hospital, but your father runs Matthews. Everyone knows that. Nothing happens in this city without the approval of Samuel Grant II. It's up to him to see that the CDC is called in. Matthews won't do it on his own."

Susannah stopped and turned to face Will on the bottom step. "You make it sound like my father is a dictator! He's not!"

"I didn't say that." Will smiled. "King, maybe." The smile faded. "You know it's true, Susannah. He could get the CDC here in no time if he wanted. And that's what he needs to do. Can't you talk him into it?"

"He called in Dr. Beck," Susannah argued. "The most famous virologist in the world."

"And has he come up with an answer?"

"Well, no, not yet, but . . ."

Someone called Susannah's name. She turned to see Zack Ballou running out of the darkness, waving at her. "There you are!" When he arrived at the foot of the steps, slightly breathless, he nodded at Will and said to Susannah, "I was hoping you'd show up at the club tonight. I wanted to know how your brother was. He's not worse, is he? Sam, isn't that his name?"

"Zack, what are you doing here? Aren't you playing tonight?"

"We're on break. I called your house, and your housekeeper said you were here. So, is Sam okay?"

"He's hanging in there."

Zack glanced up at Will, who was listening silently. "Where are you two off to?"

Susannah couldn't believe Zack had left the club to come looking for her. "There was an accident, near my house. A girl almost drowned. I rode with Will in the ambulance, so he's taking me back to my car."

"Oh, I'll do that." Zack smiled easily at Will. "No need for you to tear yourself away. I know how busy you guys are these days, what with that fever and everything. I'll take Susannah to her car. You can get back to work."

It almost sounded like an order. Will's eyes narrowed. "Well, gee, thanks," he said lazily, "but I promised Susannah I'd give her a lift, and I don't break promises. If you need to talk to her, why don't you follow us out there in your car?"

Susannah hid a smile. All of a sudden, Will was staking a claim on her? Since when?

Since a very good-looking musician had showed up, looking for her.

If Will was determined, Zack was even more so. "That'd be pretty lame. All of us driving out there in two separate cars." He looked to Susannah for support. "Right? Wouldn't it make more sense for you to come with me?"

She had to admit that it did. Besides, Will had a lot of nerve, paying no attention to her whatsoever until someone else did. And he had blamed her father for not doing more to halt the spread of the fever, when that wasn't even her father's job. That job belonged to Matthews. "Zack is right, Will. I really shouldn't take you away from the hospital. Your break is only fifteen minutes. It would take longer than that to drive all the way out the boulevard and back again. That doesn't make much sense. I'll just go with Zack, okay?"

When she saw the look on Will's lean, handsome face, she willed the words back, but it was too late. He stiffened, and his lips drew together tightly. "Sure. Whatever you say. Let's be sensible, by all means. Let us always be sensible." Then he turned and, without hurrying, walked back up the steps and disappeared inside the hospital.

Zack laughed and reached out for Susannah's hand. She let him take it and they began to walk toward the parking garage. "Looks like your paramedic is suffering from an advanced case of jealousy," he said. "You two have something going?"

"No." And until tonight, Susannah thought, I was pretty sure there wasn't any chance of that ever happening. But Will had definitely been annoyed when Zack showed up. So maybe she'd been wrong. "He's just tired. Tonight was awful. Horrible."

In Zack's rental car, speeding along Linden Hill Boulevard, she told him about the near-drowning and about Dr. Mulgrew's diagnosis of another new case of fever. "We thought we'd seen the last case," she added wearily. "And all those people at the party were exposed. We could have lots more cases now." The thought made her head ache. She wished she hadn't hurt Will's feelings. Zack would be gone soon, but Will wouldn't. She'd be working with him at Emsee. He and Kate had always been there for her when no one else was. Now she'd made him mad.

Zack pulled up beside her car in front of the Dwyer house. The street no longer looked like a parking lot, and the house was dark. Pinky and her parents were probably at the hospital waiting for word on Sally's condition. "Come back to the club with me?" he asked. "I could probably squeeze in a couple of dances."

He really was nice. It would have been fun to

go back to the club with him, relax and listen to music, dance a little. Maybe life would seem a little less grim if she went with him. If Abby shows up there, I could stay with her tonight, Susannah thought, and I wouldn't have to go home. Linden Hall is *not* going to be a happy place tonight, with everyone so worried about Sam.

But if she went back to the club, she'd keep seeing Sam out on that dance floor and the way he'd looked at her just before he fell. She couldn't stand that.

"Thanks, but I think I should go back to the hospital. My parents will probably stay there all night, and I might, too. I want Sam to know we're all pulling for him. I know he probably won't even know we're there, but . . ."

"But *you* know it," Zack finished for her in a sympathetic voice. "That's what counts, right?" He reached across her to open the car door. Instead of pushing down on the handle, he reached up, turned her face toward his, and kissed her. It was not a hasty kiss, and he didn't seem to be in a hurry to let her go. Susannah realized she didn't *want* him to let her go. Was it attraction? Fear? When he did release her, he gave her a quick smile and said, "Maybe by tomorrow night, your brother will be sitting up and eating a Quarter Pounder. Then you can come to the club, okay? I'll be waiting."

Still feeling the kiss, Susannah nodded, thanked him for the ride, and left the car.

"I'll be pulling for Sam, too, Susannah," Zack promised as she closed the door and stepped up to the curb. She was touched to the point of tears by his kindness. He was being so nice, and he hardly knew her or Sam. Well . . . that kiss hadn't felt like he hardly knew her. She found herself hoping that she would have time to see more of Zack again before he left town.

But right now, all she wanted to do was go home and take a shower and race back to the hospital. She knew it wasn't just because of Sam. It was partly that. Mostly that. But there was something else. If she didn't make things right with Will, she wouldn't get a wink of sleep. And the way things were going in Grant, anyone who worked at Emsee was going to need all the sleep they could get.

18

Callie Matthews never watched the news. Too depressing. But her mother, who seldom left the house in the evening, watched it faithfully, wanting to know what was going on in the outside world. Callie was in her room, carefully painting her long fingernails with two coats of Pink Abandon, when her mother's voice called over the intercom, "Callie! Jeremy's on television. Channel three!"

On Callie's set, plainclothes detectives were engaged in a high-speed chase across the city of Chicago. Waving one hand in the air to dry the new polish, Callie reached out with her other hand to switch channels. And there he was. Jeremy. On television! A small banner on the bottom right of the screen announced that the picture of Jeremy was "live," from Med Center's Grant Memorial. Something about him saving somebody's life.

Callie's mouth hung open. Jeremy? Had saved somebody's life? How? He wasn't a paramedic like that Jackson boy, the one who was every bit as gorgeous as Denzel Washington. Besides, Jeremy Barlow wasn't the "hero" type. That paramedic probably was. And Sam Grant was. Even Jenkins Rue, who somebody had said lived in a fishing shack but was, nevertheless, really cute and a great football player, was a better candidate for "hero" than Jeremy was. When Rue wasn't lying flat on his back in a hospital bed, of course.

Must be a mistake. The only thing Jeremy Barlow had ever saved was his stupid coin collection.

Callie turned up the volume.

"In other words," a skinny, red-haired television reporter gushed as she pushed a microphone into Jeremy's face, "if you hadn't come along when you did and noticed the girl floating unconscious in your friend's pool, she would have died."

Callie burned with envy as Jeremy nodded. She couldn't tell if he was embarrassed or thrilled to pieces to be on television. Maybe both. Jeremy was one of those people who was never sure exactly how he felt about anything. Like her own family, the Barlows never talked about feelings. Jeremy had told her that was one of his mother's most frequent complaints. "Not talking about feelings doesn't make them disintegrate," she had shouted at his father many times, according to Jeremy. "Those feelings are still *in* there, turning sour like spoiled milk. And the longer they *stay* in there, the more rancid they get, Thomas, until they become positively poisonous."

Jeremy looked very much as if he were having trouble now figuring out how he felt. He kept trying to avoid the microphone, twisting his head this way and that, but when he looked straight into the camera, Callie saw pride in his eyes.

Callie herself was having *no* trouble identifying her feelings. Jealousy, pure and simple. There was Jeremy on her television set, live, and he was a hero! He was on the news, and tomorrow morning there'd be a big story about his heroism in the newspaper. Probably a picture, too.

Her picture hadn't been in the paper along with her interview. She had asked that stupid music critic if she wanted a picture, had even offered to run home and get one. She knew exactly which one she'd get. The one from last Christmas. She'd been having an exceptionally good hair day, and she looked like a model in that green velvet dress, everyone said so. But the woman had said no, no picture. And the story in the paper had only been a few crummy lines.

Jeremy would get a bigger story. And a picture.

"We have also learned," the reporter continued, swinging the microphone away from Jeremy and meeting the camera head on, "that the nearly drowned girl is the latest victim of the mysterious, unidentified fever plaguing this city. When asked what new measures were being taken to protect the public from this scourge, hospital officials refused to comment beyond assuring this reporter that due to the complete quarantine of every case, the public is not in danger at this time. This is Andrea Gray, reporting for KMXS, channel three."

The reporter was unable to restrain a look of skepticism on her face when she said, "the public is not in danger at this time." It was that look that stirred Callie into action.

Twice this week, she had overheard her father on the telephone, arguing with Samuel Grant. It hadn't been hard to figure out why they were arguing. Ever since Sam got sick, his father had pushed for outside help. Her father refused. Bad publicity and all that. He'd only agreed to call in that guy from Germany to get Samuel Grant off his back. And she'd heard him insisting that the doctor's arrival in town be kept quiet.

Well, it hadn't been. Lots of people knew he was in town. Okay, so maybe she had mentioned it to a few people. But they would have found out anyway.

She knew her mother agreed with Sam's father. She had said, straight out, two mornings ago, that the CDC in Atlanta should be called in. Caleb Matthews, usually so gentle with his ailing wife, had snapped at her. Practically told her to mind her own business, and stormed out of the house without saying good-bye to his wife or daughter.

Even that silly reporter who'd interviewed Jeremy knew that Med Center should be doing more to stop that horrible disease from spreading.

Callie turned off the television.

"Did you see him?" Her mother's voice on the intercom. "He looked so handsome, didn't he? Even with his hair wet like that. His father must be so proud."

"Yeah, he looked great," Callie called back, but her mouth twisted in disgust. If Jeremy could get his picture in the paper, so could she. And she knew exactly how.

Her father hadn't been home to dinner one single night this week. Maybe he was working, and maybe he wasn't. All she knew was, he lived at Med Center, more than he did his own home, and that had to stop. Maybe she could kill two birds with one stone here. Get her picture in the paper and get her father back home where he belonged. He'd find another job. A better job. And in a way, she'd be as much a hero as Jeremy, because she just might be responsible for ending the awful sickness everyone was so worried about. She'd be a heroine to the whole city.

Checking to make sure her new polish job was dry, Callie picked up the telephone book on her nightstand, looked up a number, and dialed. "I'd like to leave a message for Andrea Gray, please," she said when someone answered. "My name is Callie Matthews. My father runs Med Center. Could you ask her to call me, please, when she gets back to the station? It's very important."

Satisfied, she hung up, put the phone book back, surveyed her nails, and lay down on her bed, smiling up at the ceiling. The people of Grant had a right to be protected from that awful fever. What kind of a citizen would she be if she didn't help?

Where had she put that Christmas picture?

When Susannah, her hair windblown, her face flushed from hurrying, arrived in ER, she was surprised to see Abby leaning against a wall near the nurses' station, talking to Will. They were deep in conversation, and he was looking down at her with interest.

As if she's the most fascinating conversationalist Will Jackson has ever met, Susannah thought with a sharp stab of jealousy that took her breath away. And Abby, looking perfectly adorable in denim overall shorts, a white T-shirt, and work boots with thick white socks, was smiling up at Will exactly the same way she smiled up at boys she was dancing with.

She is flirting with him! Susannah thought. Then she almost laughed. You can't possibly be shocked, she scolded mentally. Flirting is as normal for Abby as breathing is for most people. She doesn't mean it.

But it still rankled. Because this time the target of those big dark eyes and that I-really-think-you're-wonderful look was Will Jackson.

Abby looked up and saw her, hesitating in the doorway. "Oh, hi, Sooz," she called, "c'mon over! We were just talking about you." She added as Susannah arrived, "Well, we were really talking about Sam. But that's *almost* like talking about you, right? Will's mom said Sam doesn't seem to be getting any worse. That's good news, right?"

"What are you doing here so late?" Susannah asked abruptly.

"I came to get *you*. Your parents will probably stay here all night, right? Mom didn't want you spending the night in that big old mansion all by yourself. Me, either. I figured this was where you'd be, so I hopped one of the Emsee shuttles. But when I got here, Will said you'd gone off somewhere with Zack."

Susannah flushed with anger. Off somewhere with Zack? Will had made it sound like a *date*? He really must be mad at her. Well, look who was talking. Hadn't he just been enjoying every single minute of Abby's flirting? She refused to look at him, although she was acutely conscious of his presence beside her. She was also remembering the heartfelt kiss. "I didn't *go* somewhere with Zack. He just took me back to my car at the Dwyers'. You heard about Sally Kent?"

Abby nodded somberly. "Isn't it awful? But at least she's still alive, thanks to Jeremy. And Will here, of course." She beamed a smile at Will.

Susannah's teeth clamped down on her tongue. When she felt it was safe to let it go, she glanced around and asked, "Where's Jeremy?"

"He went home." Will's voice was smooth, cool. No hint of anger. But when Susannah looked up at him, she saw no sign of warmth in his eyes. "I think he wanted to make sure his dad saw him on the news. Unfortunately, Barlow's still here. We've had three cardiacs in the last hour, and he was called in on consults. I guess Jeremy went home to an empty house." He smiled at Abby. "You should have rescued him along with Susannah, Abby."

"I don't need rescuing," Susannah snapped.

Will's smile vanished. "I meant, from going home to an empty house."

"I knew what you meant." To Abby, Susannah said, "I'm just going to run up and check on Sam and my parents one more time. I'll meet you outside in ten minutes, okay?" She wanted to add, Is it safe to leave you two alone down here? but she clamped her teeth tightly together and hurried off to the elevator. They could run off and get married, for all she cared! It was *none* of her business. She and Will Jackson had never even had a date! Probably never would, either.

Her father looked tired. He was pacing back and forth in the ICU hallway, hands clasped behind his back. His tie was crooked, the red handkerchief in the breast pocket of his navy blue blazer limp. But her mother, in pale blue linen, looked as perfectly put-together as she always did. What would it take, Susannah wondered, for her to lose it, just totally lose it? And realized that she already knew the answer. Something bad happening to Sam, that's what it would take. Her mother could never handle that.

"How is he?"

Samuel shrugged. "It's this waiting. Enough to drive a person crazy. Beck hasn't come up with anything except what we already knew, which is 'a fever of undiagnosed origin.' He might as well have stayed in Germany. But he's still trying."

"He needs help," Caroline announced firmly, surprising Susannah. "You know he does, Samuel."

"If he doesn't come up with something by tomorrow morning, I'll talk to Matthews again."

"You know there's a new case," Susannah said flatly as she peered in Sam's window. He wasn't moving. She reminded herself that he was, at least, still breathing. "You must have seen them bringing Sally Kent's gurney up here."

Her mother nodded. "The Kent girl. Yes. She's in a room down the hall. The doctors aren't optimistic, but that seems to be due to her accident, not the fever itself. Her parents are frightened half out of their minds. I tried my best to console Ethel, but it was hopeless."

"They shouldn't have had a party without adult supervision," Samuel said angrily.

"Oh, for heaven's sake, Samuel, even if there'd been adults there, they wouldn't have been out by the pool. We never are when our children have a pool party." To take the sting out of her words, Caroline got up and went over to put an arm around her husband. "You're just trying to find someone to blame for all of this. But the fever isn't Ethel and David's fault, now, is it?"

"No. It isn't."

Husband and wife sat down together, holding hands.

Susannah felt a pang of envy. It would be nice to have someone to share her anxiety over Sam with, too, someone who cared about her more than anything else in the world. Zack? How could someone who traveled all the time be there for her? Will? Will cared. But as a friend. Right now, she needed more than that.

She told her parents she was staying at Abby's, and left.

On the way home, although she hadn't meant to, she heard herself saying to Abby, "I can't believe you were flirting with Will!" At first she wished she hadn't said it, and then she thought, oh, what's the difference. She was tired and upset and worried about Sam, and Abby *had* been flirting with Will.

"I wasn't! What are you talking about?"

"You were so, Abigail. I know flirting when I see it, just like I know an expert at it when I see one. You're an expert, and you were batting those big dark eyes of yours."

Abby laughed. "Susannah, you're right, I was! I *was*! I'm sorry. Honestly, I didn't mean to. It just sort of . . . happened. It's like I go on automatic pilot. Don't be mad. He *is* gorgeous, is he not? And I *am* female, am I not?" She laughed again. "You can smack me if you want to. I guess I deserve it."

Susannah laughed then, and felt some of the tension slide away. "Abby, you are hopeless. Totally. Okay, I forgive you. But if it ever happens again, we're finished."

"That's not fair! *You* refuse to make a play for him. He doesn't even know how you feel. So you can't blame anyone else for thinking of him as fair game."

Susannah pulled the Benz up in front of Abby's house and parked. "Listen to yourself! Make a play for? Fair game? That language is practically medieval. Whatever happened to 'I am woman, hear me roar'?"

Laughing, Abby jumped out of the car and waited for Susannah. "Well, *roar* then," she said when they were both walking up the lighted driveway. "Do *something* to let Will know you're interested, before some other girl snaps him up. And," she added hastily, "I'm not talking about me."

"You'd better not be."

"Actually, I was pretty disappointed when Will said you'd gone somewhere with Zack. Because I happen to think *he's* really cute, too."

"I was right," Susannah said, laughing as they entered the O'Connor house, "you are positively hopeless."

"I know." Then, cheerfully, Abby said, "Keep me in mind if you decide you'd rather have Will than Zack, okay? I'll be standing by to pick up the pieces of Zack's broken heart."

They stopped laughing when Mrs. O'Connor appeared in a white terry robe to ask them what they knew about the drowning incident at the Dwyer house.

Ten minutes away, in a house far emptier than the O'Connors', Jeremy Barlow sat alone at the breakfast bar in the kitchen, drinking a glass of orange juice and wondering why he didn't feel like the hero he was supposed to be. He had called his father's office before the reporter started their interview, to tell him to switch on channel three, but there was no answer.

Finally, he'd given up and gone home, hoping

Dr. Thomas Barlow would be waiting for him.

But there was no one there. He picked up the telephone that sat at his elbow and dialed his mother's number in San Francisco.

There was no answer.

He let it ring seventeen times.

chapter
19

When Susannah arrived home from Abby's on Saturday morning, her father was striding furiously back and forth in the living room, waving a newspaper in the air and shouting about "irresponsible journalism." She stood in the doorway, wondering What now? as he continued his tirade.

"If Caleb Matthews doesn't have any more control than this over his own daughter," he shouted as his wife sat patiently in a velvet chair beside the fireplace, "maybe he shouldn't be running a first-class medical facility! Every member of the board has called me this morning about this article, and they're all furious with Matthews. His own daughter!"

Susannah realized that her mother wasn't listening. Caroline's eyes had a glazed look, as if she were somewhere else. Probably in Sam's hospital room.

"What's Callie done?" Susannah moved across the thick white carpeting to take a seat on the brick fireplace hearth. "Or should I say, what's Callie done *now*? Did she talk to a reporter again?"

Another wave of the newspaper. "She certainly did! The whole city's going to be up in arms now, in spite of the fact that half of what was printed is pure fabrication."

"That means the other half is true," Susannah couldn't refrain from saying.

Her father sent her a reproving look. "We had our reasons for not calling in the CDC. We had the community's best interests at heart." He tossed the paper at Susannah. She caught it and spread it across her lap, reading rapidly. "Now we have no choice," Samuel said angrily. "We have to call Atlanta. I've already put in a call. What this will do to Med Center, I can't imagine. I don't *want* to imagine."

"Emsee can't be the only hospital in the world that's had to deal with a contagious disease," Caroline pointed out gently. "The people from the CDC will discover what the problem is, and they'll fix it, dear. Isn't that what they're for? And" — a wash of relief flooded her face — "they'll cure Sam. They'll cure all of the patients. Isn't that the most important thing?"

Susannah wasn't listening. She was reading. Callie had laid it on pretty thick. She'd used words like "secrecy" and "plot" and "injustice" when discussing Med Center's reluctance to call in outside help. She had described the eminent virologist Dr. Beck as "some kind of specialist from out of the country, not even an American." She had hinted that the disease was wildly contagious (That's a lie! Susannah thought angrily) and that the entire population was in imminent danger of being wiped out.

Still, she was telling the truth about Emsee not contacting the CDC, and she was right about the reason. Bad publicity. Meaning money. How had Callie known that? Her father wouldn't have admitted it openly, would he? That would be a pretty stupid thing to do if Callie was anywhere within earshot.

"People are going to panic," she said grimly when she had finished reading. "The phones are going to be ringing off the hook at every hospital in the complex. I'd better get down there. One thing I can do is answer phones." Addressing her father, she asked, "So, can I tell people you are calling in the CDC? It might make them feel better. Is that a done deal?"

"Yes. You can tell them. If it will calm their fears, that might be best. The last thing we need right now is a mass panic. Tell them."

Susannah ran to change her clothes and drive to Emsee.

* * *

Saturday was another nightmare for all medical complex personnel. The phones in every hospital, including Rehab and Psych, rang incessantly. While Susannah and every other volunteer answered phones, nurses and doctors were forced to waste valuable time dissuading frightened relatives from yanking patients out of the hospitals. At the same time, Grant residents began pouring into ER, convinced their temperatures had suddenly skyrocketed and absolutely certain that they were coming down with the dreaded fever. Meanwhile, there were the usual number of valid emergencies: broken bones, heart attacks, deep lacerations requiring sutures, near-drownings in summer pools, heat stroke, highway accident victims, and accidental poisonings. ER was filled to overflowing. Doctors, nurses, orderlies, and aides raced around like marathon runners. People began shouting angrily when their needs weren't immediately met. Personnel from Social Services and Public Relations were called on to help quell the crowd's anger, but for the most part, their voices fell on deaf ears. Inflamed by Callie's printed quotes about "secrecy" and "dreaded plague," the citizens of Grant were in no mood to be placated.

It got worse. By two o'clock that afternoon, there were several dozen people marching up and down outside in the center of the complex, bearing placards and signs that read, among other things, LIFE IS MORE IMPORTANT THAN MONEY and GREEDY MED CENTER. The worst sign Susannah saw read: MED CENTER DOESN'T CARE ABOUT LIFE.

When Susannah went looking for Kate, Will told her brusquely, "She's upstairs, on five." She could tell he hadn't thawed yet. He was still ticked about Zack. She was tempted briefly to explain, then decided against it. What exactly was she supposed to explain? She wasn't about to say to him, "It's really you I care about, not Zack," when Will had never said he was interested. What did he think she was, a mind reader?

The crowd had thinned some. But every treatment room was occupied, and people still milling about in the waiting room complained loudly that they'd been waiting "hours" to have their temperatures taken. The phone on the reception desk in the lobby began jiggling shrilly. The nurse stationed there threw up her hands in despair.

Susannah turned her back on Will and wove her way through the crowded hallway to begin answering phone calls again.

Upstairs in ICU, Kate stood outside Damon Lawrence's room. He was still on a respirator and he had no visitors. A nurse wearing protective garb was adjusting an IV. There was no one else in the room. No mother sitting in a wooden chair beside the bed or leaning against the wall praying that her son would get better. Damon's mother was dead. Which was maybe one reason he'd always spent so much time at the Thompson house when he was growing up. Kate had no idea where his father was. He had once worked at the lab, but she vaguely remembered that he'd been fired for missing too many days. A drinking problem, she thought. Hadn't Will told her that a long time ago? Maybe Mr. Lawrence wasn't even around anymore.

Was Damon on his own? How awful. To be so sick and not have anyone around who cared.

Impulsively, Kate whirled around and went to the nurses' station. "I'd like to see Damon Lawrence, please."

"Sorry. No visitors."

"I'm his sister."

The nurse, busy doing paperwork, glanced up. "Oh, you are not," she said blithely. "I know you. You're Astrid Thompson's daughter, Kate, and you are *not* related to Damon Lawrence. So forget it."

"He's my half brother," Kate persisted. "My mother was married twice."

"No, she wasn't. I went to school with her, right here in Grant, and to the University with her after that. Astrid Thompson never had eyes for anyone but your father. So cut it out, okay?" Then, relenting, she added, "You're obviously a friend of the Lawrence boy. But you know the drill. Family only, and then only in protective gear and for only two minutes at a time."

"That's just it. I *do* know the drill. I know exactly what to wear and exactly how far away to stand and I know better than to touch anything. So I'm really a better visitor than family members might be, right?" Kate leaned over the desk. "Look, he's all alone in there. Has he had any visitors at all? Any?"

The nurse consulted the log. "No. Not one. But you're *not* related, Kate. If anyone found out I let you in, I'd be in big trouble."

"We're *all* in big trouble, thanks to this awful disease, whatever it is." Kate stood up straight again. "Hasn't Tina's death made you stop and think about what's important and what isn't? I mean, really, what's so great about a rule that says a boy has to lie dying all alone? That's not right, is it?"

The nurse thought about that for a minute. "He's not even going to know you're in there," she said then.

"Right. But *I'll* know. And you'll know. Won't that make you feel good, knowing he's not in there all by himself, just for a few minutes?"

If the nurse had been older, more experienced, and possibly more cynical, the approach might not have worked. But Kate could see that the idea of doing something that might make her feel good appealed to her. She'd probably had a horrible week. "Please?" Kate pleaded.

"Oh, all right. But you suit up, and don't forget your goggles. We still don't know how this thing spreads. Two minutes, Kate, no more!"

"I promise."

As she donned the awkward gear, Kate had no idea why she'd been so persistent about seeing Damon. He'd been a great kid when he was little, but then he'd changed. They weren't close friends anymore. She didn't even know who his friends were these days. Probably people she didn't want to know. Tough kids, probably, maybe even mean.

But when she got inside and stood beside Damon's bed, he looked anything but tough or mean. There is, she thought, gazing down at him, something so helpless and innocent about a critically ill person. The illness takes over, swallowing up every last trace of who they really are, until all you see is the illness itself. With his eyes closed and his features relaxed, Damon looked so much like the little boy she'd known a long time ago that she felt a lump in her throat.

Tentatively, Kate reached out and touched his

hand with her gloved one. "What happened to you, Damon?" she asked softly. "Before the fever, I mean. Where did you go?"

She was still standing there, still touching his hand, when the nurse opened the door and stuck her head in. "Kate," she said quietly, "time's up. Come on out."

Reluctantly, Kate turned and left the room.

chapter
20

Upstairs in his office, Caleb Matthews, a newspaper lying open on his desk, tried once again to reach his daughter by telephone. The chaos downstairs in ER was her fault, all her fault. This outrageous article in the paper . . . what had got into her? How could she betray her own father like that? If he held on to his job, it would be a miracle. His teeth clenched as the phone went unanswered. He slammed down the receiver. "If I get my hands on that girl . . ."

In her bedroom at home, his daughter lay on her back on the pink carpet, holding an open newspaper above her head. She smiled as she turned the newspaper this way and that, examining from every angle the photograph of herself in the green velvet dress. Pleased with what she saw, she then read the article again, her lips moving as if she were actually saying the words aloud.

Two floors above Caleb Matthews's office in the Emergency Services building, a short blonde secretary entered a large, lavish office. The huge picture window behind an enormous mahogany desk provided a clear view of one half of Med Center. A tall, youthful-looking man with prematurely graying hair sat at the desk, reading. The secretary smiled as she entered, carrying the day's mail, and approached the desk. She placed the packet of mail on the desk and said, "Congratulations, Dr. Barlow! You must be so proud. Having a hero for a son!"

The doctor lifted his head, keeping an index finger on his place in the medical journal article. "Excuse me? What's this about a hero?"

"Oh, Dr. Barlow, don't be modest. I'm talking about Jeremy, of course. Saving that girl's life. My goodness, I would think you'd be bursting your buttons with pride. I would be, if it were my son."

Confusion filled the doctor's face. "Saved a life? Jeremy?"

The secretary looked surprised, then just as confused as the doctor. "You didn't hear about it? But it was on the news and in the paper this morning. With a wonderful picture of Jeremy. Such a nice-looking boy. I wouldn't be surprised if one of those news magazine shows got hold of the story and decided to go national with it. People do so like to hear good news. Especially these days."

When the doctor continued to look blank, the woman went on talking, slowly, one sentence at a time, as if she expected him to say at any moment, "Oh, yes, now I remember!" But he didn't say that. "The Kent girl," she told him, "almost drowned at a party last night. Your son jumped in and pulled her out. He gave her CPR until Fire and Rescue arrived." Still, the doctor said nothing. He was listening, she could tell, but he didn't seem to be taking in what she was saying. He looked blank. "Everyone in the hospital's talking about it. I can't believe he didn't tell you."

"Last night, you say? I got home late. I had a late dinner at the Club with some friends. I assumed my son was already in bed. I had early surgery this morning, so I was out of the house before he woke up. I haven't actually seen him since . . . well, it's been a day or two. Busy, you know, with everything's that's been going on. This place has been a zoo." The doctor leaned back in his expensive leather chair, folded his hands in his lap, and, still looking confused, murmured, "Jeremy? *My* Jeremy?"

"So, has your mom canceled the fashion show?" Abby asked Susannah when they met after work. "You said you thought she should."

Susannah was exhausted, and for the first time since she'd begun volunteering, thankful to be leaving Emsee. "I don't know. I guess so." The marchers with picket signs had gone. The grass where they'd walked, and then tusseled, looked bruised. "This was the worst day I've had since I started here. All those people. Everyone in town is scared to death. No one would come here for the fashion show even if we did have it."

"Tons of people called to cancel surgery at Memorial that they'd had scheduled for weeks. I told every single one of them that all of the fever patients were off in Isolation in your building, but they wouldn't change their minds. At least a dozen patients were yanked out of Psych this afternoon, taken somewhere else by relatives. All of the routine tests that were supposed to be done at the lab have been canceled, too."

"I guess my father was right," Susannah said gloomily. "He said this would happen if the word got out, and now it's happening." She hated the thought of Med Center's image being tarnished in this way. It was easy enough to accuse people of panicking needlessly, but could she really blame them? She understood why they were so frightened. She'd read the article, too. "Why do *you* think Callie did it? I mean, the language she used was so scary. 'Deadly plague,' for instance. Eight cases do not make a plague, and she knows that. It's like she was deliberately trying to scare people. That's so mean."

"How are the others?" Abby wanted to know. "How's Jenkins? And I heard Damon was on a respirator. That's a bad sign, right? Sam isn't that bad, is he? Did you see him today?"

"No, he isn't any worse. They're all hanging in there. It's kind of weird, when you think about it." They reached the Benz and climbed in. "I mean, I couldn't be happier that they're all still alive. But after Tina died, I guess we all thought everyone who got it would die, too. But they're all still with us. Damon is the sickest, but even he is still hanging on. So whatever this thing is, it isn't necessarily fatal, the way we thought at first. Callie had no business hinting that it was. Scaring people like that."

"And making it sound like the most treacherous, uncaring, perfidious people in the world work at Med Center," Abby agreed. "That's hard to forgive."

"Especially when it was mostly her own father who refused to call the CDC."

"And yours," Abby reminded gently.

Susannah sighed. "Yeah, I know. But at least he's doing something constructive now. I hope," she added fervently.

He had. When Susannah arrived home, so tired she walked up the wide, stone steps to Linden Hall slowly, like one of the arthritic patients at Rehab, she found a guest in the library with her father.

He called out to her as she passed the open doorway, "Susannah, I'm glad you're home! I want you to meet someone." The look he gave her as she entered the room clearly said, See? I've done what you've asked. "This is Dr. Leora Cicero from the Centers for Disease Control in Atlanta. This is my daughter, Susannah. We've already talked about her twin, you remember."

Susannah smiled at the tall, thin woman in the navy blue suit, and extended her hand. "I can't tell you how glad I am that you're here." A small, tired laugh escaped her. "And I can't tell you how much I mean that." She noticed then that Dr. Beck was also in the room, and sent him a wave in greeting.

The woman smiled. "I know you've all been very worried. We don't know yet what this is you've been dealing with, but we intend to find out."

We? Susannah quickly glanced around the room. Was she referring to herself and Dr. Beck?

Seeing the glance, Dr. Cicero said, "I have a partner, Dr. Link. He's on a tour of your mother's rose garden." She smiled. "I'm allergic, or I would have gone, too." Then she added with concern, "You look exhausted. You're feeling all right?"

"Oh, sure," Susannah said hastily, seeing the fear that sprang into her father's eyes at the question. "I'm fine. I'm just . . . it was pretty hairy today at ER, because of that article in the paper this morning. I'm a little tired, that's all. Will you be staying here with us?"

"Of course they will, Susannah," her father

answered for the doctor. "Now, if you'll excuse us, we'd like to continue our discussion."

Susannah had been looking forward to a long, hot shower and maybe a quick nap before returning to the hospital to visit Sam. But she hadn't anticipated being in the company of a medical investigator from the CDC. It was such a wonderful opportunity to learn. "Could I stay, please? I'd like to know what's going on."

Her father shook his head no, but Dr. Cicero said, "Of course. The illness has struck down a member of your family, so naturally you're interested." She smiled again. Susannah realized that the doctor was only a plain woman until she smiled. Then she was very pretty. "And I'm told you work at Med Center, Susannah, so you're practically a colleague. I think you should stay."

When Dr. Cicero's partner had returned from the rose garden, Susannah had no trouble staying awake to listen to the conversation. She was eager to hear what, if anything, Dr. Beck had discovered.

Not much, apparently. It wasn't hemorrhagic fever, that was clear, he said, because there were no signs of bleeding. Nor was it any known type of influenza. Although, he added, it could still be an entirely new strain.

When he had told them all of the things that the fever wasn't, Dr. Cicero asked, "So, what's your best guess so far?"

Susannah leaned forward to catch Dr. Beck's answer. "My best guess," he said in his very formal English, "is that what we are dealing with is a brand-new virus, one that has never surfaced before in this country."

chapter
21

"**T**ests show that it isn't typhoid, dengue, malaria, or influenza," Dr. Beck continued, "nor is it any other known arboviral, enteroviral, or adenoviral infection. I believe there is every reason to suspect something new and unknown."

Susannah expected Dr. Cicero to look disheartened by the news. Instead, she seemed intrigued. "None of the current patients have recently traveled out of the country?"

Dr. Beck shook his head no.

"Then we'll begin," the CDC investigator said briskly, "with a massive media campaign."

Samuel Grant audibly drew in his breath. Susannah could almost feel shock waves coming from him. "Media?"

"Yes, of course. The disease originated out of this country, that much I'm sure of. What we probably have on our hands is one of the new viruses that seem to be popping up more frequently as we move into more remote corners of the world. Since none of the patients had traveled recently, we must use the media to ask that people from this area who have been out of the country come forward to be tested for the virus. And then we must hope there will be a survivor who is a native of this country, rather than someone who was just visiting and might already have returned home."

When no one said anything, the doctor continued, "We will, of course, use our computers to inquire about recent, unexplained fever deaths in other countries. But if the source of this disease came from some remote village, that information may not be available to us. So, what we need is someone who survived the fever and is available to us. A resident of this area, preferably. He probably didn't even realize what he had. And we must hope that he will respond to our media request to come forward and be tested."

"That's a lot of if's," Samuel said grudgingly.

Dr. Cicero stood up, signaling to her partner, Dr. Link, a young man with thinning hair and very thick glasses, to do the same. "Yes, it is," she admitted. "But there are always a lot of questions in a situation like this. Our job is to find the answers. We will do that, Mr. Grant, if there is an answer to be found."

"Another if."

"Yes. Possibly the most important one. Meanwhile, I want everyone at Med Center tested, right down to the least important delivery person."

"All of the medical personnel have been tested," Dr. Beck said as he stood up.

"Test them again. Also administration, clerical, maintenance, delivery people, everyone. And everyone at the University, as well. We have no idea what the incubation period of this disease is. These people who tested negative last week could be positive now. What we are primarily interested in just now is anyone who might have been out of the country recently."

Susannah had been listening quietly. Now she said slowly, "I think I might know some people who've been out of the country." Zack Ballou had told her the band occasionally traveled internationally. "I don't know how recently. And they were sick on their last trip. But I don't know when that was. They thought it was the water."

Dr. Cicero nodded. "It probably was. Still, we must check." Susannah gave him Zack's name. He wrote it down on a yellow pad.

Dr. Cicero nodded and made notes, too.

"Well, there's Montgomery, too," Samuel reluctantly said then. "Leonard Montgomery. My man from the lab. Recently returned from a trip to South America. It was his daughter who died. But," he added quickly, "he wasn't sick."

Dr. Cicero and Dr. Link looked interested. "Where in South America?" Link asked.

"Brazil. Although. . . ." Samuel paused.

Susannah knew how much her father did *not* want one of his employees to be responsible for the fever. Because that would almost make *him* responsible.

"Yes?" Dr. Cicero prompted.

"Although *he* stayed in the city, the people he contacted while he was there were from a small village in a remote area, a place called Esperanza. I know that it took them a long time to make the trip to meet with Montgomery. But," he added quickly, "he would have told me if any of them were sick."

"He has been tested?"

"No, not yet. He's Administration. We tested the medical personnel."

More note-taking. It seemed to Susannah, watching carefully, that all three doctors looked optimistic. But that could be, she told herself, because it's how I want them to look. Optimistic. Like they're going to get to the bottom of this very quickly. And fix it.

When Samuel had agreed to take the doctors to the lab at Grant Pharmaceuticals and led them from the room, Caroline turned to Susannah. There were new worry lines around her eyes and mouth. "I have postponed the fashion show. Would you mind calling your friends who were modeling and telling them? I have so many other calls to make, and I really want to get back to the hospital. Tell them I had no choice but to postpone. The musicians I had hired canceled, as did the florist. No one wants to come near Med Center just now. I don't blame them." Then, in the same tone of voice, Caroline added, "And, of course, you're not to go near there, either, Susannah. Except to visit Sam. No volunteering, not now. It's simply too dangerous."

Susannah stared at her. "You're kidding!"

Her mother returned the stare. "Kidding? Why would I be kidding? I'm quite serious." She reached up to adjust her gold necklace absent-mindedly. "I have one child in the hospital already, Susannah. Isn't that enough?"

"Mother, I'm not staying away from Emsee. Not now. They need all the help they can get. We've had a lot of people from Grant volunteering, but we've also had staff and maintenance workers calling in sick. They're not really sick. They're scared. So we're understaffed, and the phones ring constantly. I can't stay home."

Caroline drew herself up to her full height, two inches taller than her daughter. "Yes. You can. And you will. I don't want to discuss this now, Susannah. I must go say good-bye to our guests." She turned and began striding from the room.

"Mother!" When was the last time her mother had given her an order? Susannah couldn't remember that far back. Caroline turned only halfway around, glancing over her shoulder at her daughter, indicating that she wasn't prepared to stop and talk. "Mother, I know you're scared. We all are. I promise I'll be careful, but I am going back down there."

"No. You are not." Then she was gone, leaving Susannah standing in the center of the room in front of the fireplace with her mouth open.

She stood there for several minutes, feeling as shocked as her father must have felt when Dr. Cicero had mentioned a media campaign. Not go back to Emsee? Now? When she was so needed? When she was actually being allowed to be of some use?

Recovering from the shock of her mother's order, she turned and walked swiftly to the telephone. "Abby?" she began when her ring was answered. "Abby, I'm coming over there. Can I stay all night? And maybe tomorrow night and the next night, in fact, maybe forever, because I might not ever be allowed to come home again. Can I come?"

She quickly changed into a black miniskirt and a black-and-white-striped crop top and black flats, piled her hair carelessly on top of her head, and began packing an overnight bag. She hastily stuffed the black bag with T-shirts and a clean pair of jeans and four pairs of white socks and a heavy sweater in case the nights got cold, her alarm clock, and a blue denim skirt and two white blouses in case she really did have to stay at

Abby's forever. She was crying tears of fury and frustration as she moved into the bathroom to angrily snatch up her toothbrush and toothpaste, makeup and a can of mousse. "I know she's worried," she muttered to herself as she traveled back and forth across the rose-colored carpet fetching and carrying, "but I'm not a child. I can take care of myself! Since when does she give me orders? Anyway, I'm not a coward, and she shouldn't want me to be one. I'm not afraid of that disease. If *everyone* was, who would take care of the patients at Emsee? Who would take care of Sam?"

She would have asked that of Caroline if she'd run into her on her way out of the house, but she didn't. And she didn't want to go hunting for her. Neither one of them was in any shape for a real battle. It could wait.

She scribbled a note on the pad beside the telephone in the front hall and left the house, wishing she had the Jeep instead of the Benz. Who ever heard of someone running away from home in a Mercedes-Benz? It seemed almost as ludicrous as being driven away in a chauffered limousine.

At the O'Connor house, Abby was waiting for her, sitting on the lawn at the edge of the driveway in the deepening twilight, one red-sweatshirted arm around her brother Mattie, the other around the old dog, Lazybones. She climbed to her feet as Susannah got out of the car, toting the overnight bag.

"Hey, what's up? You and your dad have a fight?"

"Guess again. Me and my mother."

"You're kidding!" Abby knew how lax Caroline was about discipline. "What about?"

Susannah told her as they walked up to the house.

"She's scared about Sam, Sooz."

"I know. I'm not mad at her anymore. But I'm not staying away from Emsee, either. In fact" — she glanced at Abby as they entered the house — "I was thinking of going over there tonight. Interested?"

"I thought you were beat."

"I was. But I feel better now that the CDC is in town, and I know how short-staffed they are in ER. Want to come along?"

"You know how I feel about ER." They hurried down the hall to Abby and Moira's room, where Susannah deposited her bag and flopped down on one of the twin beds. Abby sat on the hardwood floor. "Besides, I was hoping I could talk you into going to The Music Room tonight."

"You're kidding! Dancing? How can you dance when the whole town has turned against the hospital? When everyone in Grant is scared to death of getting sick?"

Abby looked genuinely puzzled. "What's that

got to do with anything? People aren't mad at us. And we're not sick." She lay down on her back, propping her legs, in black leggings, up on the edge of her bed. "Don't you care about Zack at all? With people hiding in their houses to avoid the fever, hardly anyone will be at The Music Room. He'll feel bad. He'll think people don't like his band. Maybe the manager will think the same thing, and fire them." Smiling shyly, Abby added, "Will's going. So is Kate. They like the band, they don't think it's fair that the fever is ruining business for Zack, and they want to show their support."

"Are you sure?"

"I promise. Kate called earlier, wanted to know if we were going. She said all of the ER night shift people showed up for work, so they're not understaffed tonight. Come on, Susannah, you worked over there all day long. So did I. We deserve a break."

Susannah was tempted. It could be the perfect opportunity to make things right with Will. Unless . . . unless Zack got in the way again.

That thought surprised her. Zack was in the way? Cute, talented Zack, who had been so understanding? In the way of what?

But she knew of what. Of any chance for her to have a relationship with Will. And that was what she wanted. What she didn't know was if he wanted that, too.

"Okay, I'll go." Susannah stood up, picking up her overnight bag and slinging it over her shoulder. "But I need a shower first. My hair feels like straw. And I want to stop at Emsee on the way and check on Sam." In the doorway, she stopped and said over her shoulder, "Abby, remember you told me that if I wasn't interested in Zack to let you know? Well, I say go for it!"

Abby grinned with delight. "Really?"

"Really." Susannah felt compelled to add, "I have to warn you, though, there's a chance that the band might be responsible for the fever." At the look of alarm on Abby's face, Susannah added hastily, "I mean, maybe not. But the doctors from the CDC think this is a new virus, something that probably came in from another country. And Zack said they sometimes travel internationally. He even said the band had been sick on one of those trips. They could have had the virus without knowing it and brought it here. I guess the CDC is looking into it. I thought you should know."

Abby thought about that for a minute or two. "You danced with him, and you don't have it."

"True. But no one knows how long it takes to get it after you've been exposed." She had danced with Zack over a week ago. And . . . he had kissed her. If he really was spreading the fever, wouldn't she have some sign of the disease by now?

Abby thought again. Then, grinning, her dark eyes sparkling with mischief, she said, "Tell you what. I won't kiss him, okay? Not tonight."

Susannah remained uncertain. "You could wait and see what the CDC finds out when they test him and the other band members. Before you make a move on him, I mean."

Abby's grin widened. "Right. The guy is only going to be here another week and you expect me to wait. I've already wasted most of this week because of your mother's fashion show and because I thought *you* wanted him for yourself. I say, seize the moment, that's what *I* say."

"Okay, okay. But don't say I didn't warn you."

"I won't say you didn't warn me. Go take your shower."

Although the shower was relaxing in spite of various O'Connor offspring knocking on the bathroom door every few minutes, Susannah felt her neck muscles tensing again as she dried her hair. Maybe she shouldn't have agreed to go to The Music Room. If she'd refused, Abby would have stayed home, too. She wouldn't go without Susannah.

Here I am, Susannah thought, angry with herself, encouraging my best friend to get friendly with someone I *know* was out of the country, and even got sick while he was there. That doesn't mean he had the virus, or that he brought it into Grant, but it *could*. Why don't I just give her a bomb to play with?

An hour later, as they drove first to Emsee and then, when Susannah had learned that there was no change in Sam's condition, to The Music Room, they found the streets of Grant eerily quiet and deserted. As if, Susannah thought nervously, the fever had already stripped the city of life.

It wasn't going to *do* that, was it?

chapter
22

The Music Room, when Susannah and Abby arrived, was as empty as a store at closing time. But it wasn't closing time. It was only nine o'clock, and on a Saturday evening at that hour, the club should have been noisy and lively.

Kate and Will were seated, by themselves, at a table close to the bandstand. At another table on the opposite side of the room, Jeremy sat with, to Susannah's dismay, Callie Matthews, vibrant in a black strapless dress very different from the casual clothes Abby and Susannah were wearing. The pair didn't look like they were having a good time. Susannah said as much to Abby.

"How could anyone have a good time with *her*?" Abby replied, casting a look of scorn Callie's way. "Jeremy shouldn't even be speaking to her, after that horrible interview she gave to the paper. His father's a doctor. Didn't he ever warn his son to stay away from poison?"

There were a few other tables occupied, but not many. Susannah knew why. The crowd usually in this club, dancing and having fun, was on average, the same age as all but one of the fever victims now in Intensive Care Isolation. They were scared. If they hadn't been at first, the collapse of a formerly healthy speciman like Samuel Grant III right in front of their very eyes, in this same club, must have erased the last bit of doubt that they were at risk.

They weren't taking any chances.

Abby and Susannah joined Kate and Will at their table.

Susannah felt sorry for Zack, who looked very dejected up there on stage. He didn't look sick, though. She wondered if anyone else in the room, besides Abby, knew that he was going to be interviewed and tested by the CDC tomorrow, and quickly decided no one did.

Though she felt sorry for him, she danced with him only once, and when he asked her to a movie on Sunday night when the club was closed, she said no.

He was surprised, she could tell. "You're busy?" he asked.

"No . . . yes . . . I . . ." Her eyes went to Will, deep in conversation with Kate and Abby at the table.

Zack followed her glance. "Oh. Gotcha. That explains the other night." He laughed, a not unfriendly sound. "He sure was ticked! I couldn't figure out why. Now I know."

Afraid Zack would say something to Will, she

said quickly, "Well, we're not . . . I mean, nothing's . . . we're not dating or anything. He's never even asked me to dance."

"But he didn't say no when you asked him to dance, did he?"

"Oh, I've never asked . . ." Susannah flushed as Zack grinned at her. She nodded and echoed his, "Gotcha! But I think he's mad at me now."

"So, ask him to dance and maybe he'll get over it. I can tell you for a fact that I'd get over my mad pretty fast for a chance to dance with you."

"Abby's a better dancer than I am," Susannah said quickly as he led her back to the table.

"Abby? The one with the eyes?"

Susannah laughed. "We all have eyes, Zack."

"You know what I mean. Big brown eyes. I had a springer spaniel with eyes like that when I was a kid." He smiled down at Susannah as she took a seat beside Kate. Then he turned to Abby. "Feel like making a fool of yourself by dancing when there's no one else out on the dance floor?"

"I hate crowds," she said, and got up to follow him out onto the floor.

Susannah felt Will's eyes on her as Zack and Abby left the table. But he continued his conversation with Kate. "It's worse than that," he was saying. "We had a cardiac arrest today, downtown, right in front of Sturgess's department store. When we got there, the guy was lying in the middle of the sidewalk, with a dozen or more people standing around. But no one had loosened his collar or put anything under his head, and no one was attempting CPR. They were all scared he had the fever. Man, it chilled my blood. The guy could have died. He didn't, but no thanks to all those people."

"They're not the only ones who are scared," Kate replied. "Look at this place! It's practically deserted. It's rough at home, too. My brother Aaron didn't speak to anyone at dinner tonight, he's so furious with my mother and me for continuing to work at Emsee. He's terrified we'll bring the fever home. Mom said she was going to talk to him, but I don't think it'll do any good."

"The investigators from the CDC are here," Susannah announced, optimism in her voice. "They seem to know what they're doing. Maybe we'll have an answer soon . . . and a vaccine. Will, would you like to dance?"

Will and Kate stared at her. Susannah couldn't tell which had surprised them more, her announcement about the CDC people arriving, or her invitation to Will. She was betting it was the invitation.

When Will didn't respond immediately, Kate said dryly, "Will, I think someone just asked you to dance."

"Someone did," Susannah said boldly. "Me. And I'm still waiting for a yes or no."

"Yes," Will said then, getting up and coming over to stand beside her chair.

Susannah left her chair and led the way to the dance floor. "I thought you were going to say no," she said when she was in his arms in a slow dance. "You took long enough answering me."

"That's what I always thought about you," he said, his chin on the top of her head. "That you'd say no. That's why I never asked."

"I wouldn't have said no."

"I didn't know that. And even if I'd thought you would say yes, there's always your father."

"Oh, he'd definitely say no if you asked him to dance," Susannah said seriously, but she was smiling, her cheek against Will's blue denim shirt.

He laughed. "You know what I mean. If your father has a list of requirements for the perfect guy for his daughter, and I'll bet he does, 'white' is probably at the very top."

"Doesn't matter. I ran away from home tonight. I'm staying at Abby's."

He reached down with one hand and lifted her chin so that she was looking straight into his eyes. "Are you serious?"

"Sort of. My mother and I had an argument. She ordered me to stay away from Emsee, and I can't do that. So I'm staying at Abby's."

"Your mother? Not your father?"

"Nope. It was my mother this time. Big surprise. It's so unlike her, giving orders. She's scared about Sam, that's all. But I'm staying out of her way until this is over. I'll have to visit Sam when my parents are taking a coffee break downstairs."

"I'm sorry you're having a rough time," he said quietly.

He was *so* nice. "Thanks," she said quietly. This was what she had wished for, after all. Someone to understand what she was feeling, how scared she was. She moved closer, lay her cheek against his shoulder. It felt warm and solid. She was dancing with Will, something she'd dreamed of for a long time. They were good together, she could feel it. They moved across the floor almost like one person.

She lifted her head, looked up at him. "You didn't ask me to dance before this because you thought I'd say no?"

"That's exactly what I thought," he said firmly.

"Well, don't ever use that as an excuse again, okay?"

"Gotcha. Now quit looking at me like that. It makes me want to kiss you, and I don't think that's a good idea. Not here. Not now."

Smiling, Susannah lay her head back against his shoulder.

They were just returning to the table when Caleb Matthews, looking flushed and anxious, appeared in the doorway. Susannah saw him come in. She watched as he strode quickly across the room to Callie and Jeremy's table.

The room was so empty and quiet, everyone could hear clearly as Matthews said to his daughter. "You were grounded! Because of the mess you've made of things with that newspaper article. I thought you were home with your mother! You have to come, now! She's sick. She's very sick."

Callie looked up at him with cool eyes. "She's sick? She was asleep when I left the house. She seemed okay." She thought for a minute, twirling the glass in her hand. Then she looked up at her father and asked, "You can handle it, right?" Sarcasm coated her words. "You're so good at handling things. Of course, you don't know the routine when she has one of these attacks as well as I do, because you're never around when she has them. But it's not that complicated, really. Take her to the ER. They'll know what to do."

"She's already at the ER." Callie's father's voice was cold. "I took her there. But it's not an attack." He reached down and grabbed Callie's left arm, yanking her out of the chair and upright. "You're coming with me. Your mother is very ill. You should be there."

Callie glared at him. "What's wrong with her?"

Susannah, listening, knew what he was going to say even before the words slid from his mouth. Her heart stopped and her breath caught in her throat. No, please, she thought, please don't let him say it! Please let me be wrong.

She wasn't wrong.

"Your mother has the same fever that killed Tina," Caleb Matthews told his daughter, his voice harsh. "She's one of three new cases that were brought into the ER tonight."

Then he threw Callie's black-sequined sweater around her shoulders and hurried her out of the nearly deserted club.

chapter
23

At the words "three new cases," The Music Room emptied out fast. Susannah, Will, Kate, Abby, and Jeremy all followed the Matthews car to Med Center. If things had gone from bad to worse at ER, the three volunteers and the paramedic wanted to be there to help. Jeremy went hoping to provide moral support for Callie.

ER was chaotic. Word had already spread of the three new cases. People who had been placated earlier that day by the news that CDC investigators had arrived had panicked anew, descending upon Med Center en masse. They filled the waiting rooms and the hallways, making it difficult for orderlies and paramedics pushing gurneyed patients to get through to treatment rooms.

"Why haven't they *done* anything?" a tall, husky friend of Jenkins Rue shouted, waving a fist in the air. "How come it's still spreading?"

A woman with pink foam rollers poking out from beneath her red print head scarf cried, "My kids aren't safe! I thought you said this afternoon that my kids would be safe! But now we've got these new cases."

The young boy at her side echoed, "Yeah, and I don't wanta get it!"

"What a mess!" Susannah murmured as she stood in the doorway with Will, surveying the scene in dismay. Kate, Abby, and Jeremy were behind them, commenting on the chaos.

Off to one side of the packed hallway, Callie Matthews stood, arguing with her father. In spite of the buzz of anger coming from the crowd, the voices of father and daughter rang clearly throughout the hall.

"That's why you gave that hateful interview?" Mr. Matthews, his face lined with weariness and worry, asked his daughter in a loud voice. "But I told you, you were wrong about that! I explained. I was telling the truth, Callie. Your mother is the most important person in the world to me."

People became aware that something was happening, and the crowd gradually fell silent, listening.

"Then why aren't you ever home?" Callie shouted. A diminutive figure dressed in sophisticated black, her fair hair hanging down her back, she looked ready for battle. Her voice rang out in the corridor. Nurses frantically trying to field phone calls held the receivers away from them, tilting their heads, their interest piqued. "Why would you rather be here than there, with us?" Her voice lowered slightly. "I can't do it all by myself. It's hard, when she's sick half the time. . . ."

"That's the girl who let us know what was going on," someone in the crowd said loudly. "I recognize her from her picture. She's the only one who would tell us the truth."

It *wasn't* the truth, Susannah wanted to shout. But she couldn't, because *half* of it *was* the truth.

"You tell 'im, Callie!" someone shouted, and there was sporadic applause from the crowd. Other voices shouted support, urging her on.

Callie paid no attention. She was completely caught up in the confrontation with her father. She hated him. This was all his fault. His and Med Center's and the Grants'. "If you'd told the truth about this from the start," she cried, looking up at him, "if you'd called in outside help immediately, maybe Mom wouldn't have the fever now!"

Her father's face drained completely of color. "Callie, don't say that! Don't *say* that!" he cried.

"She could *die*, Dad," Callie pressed on relentlessly. "She's not strong like the other people who have it. You know she's not."

"I've been keeping a very close watch on her, Callie. I was worried about the fever, too. And I brought her in the very second she felt the least bit warm. Dr. Mulgrew said she couldn't have had a temperature for more than a few hours. Look, we have to be there for your mother, both of us."

Watching, Susannah felt a pang of sympathy for the man. Abby must have, too, because she murmured, "Oh, damn it, Callie, give him a hug!" Even the angry crowd, who knew now that the big man in the light blue sweater, standing against the wall with his head down, was one of the targets of their anger, had hushed and seemed to be holding its breath. Powerful though the man might be, he, too, was now a victim of the indiscriminating fever, and it was clear to all that he was in great pain. Maybe that was punishment enough.

"I know she's spoiled," Jeremy said softly as he watched and waited with everyone else to see what Callie would do, "but she's not heartless."

Callie had never felt so torn. She was still so angry with her father. But his face was twisted in pain, and there were tears in his eyes. "You really love Mom?" she asked, her voice softening just a little.

He nodded. "And you, too, Callie."

"You care about us?"

"I do. Very much."

Callie nodded. She didn't hug him. But she nodded again and said, "Okay. Then let's go up and see how she is."

Abby, watching, knew Callie's softening was

only temporary. Callie, after all, was Callie. Caleb Matthews appeared to be satisfied, however, as if he hadn't dared hope for even that much from his daughter.

The elevator doors slid open. Father and daughter disappeared inside.

Jeremy made his way through the crowd to follow them upstairs.

The drama over, people returned to their own concerns. They remembered why they were there and why they were angry. Voices began clamoring once again to have temperatures taken, to be taken directly to the CDC investigators, to be given a hospital bed immediately because they were feeling "very, very sick."

It was, finally, Susannah's father who cleared the waiting rooms and corridors. An orderly had gone upstairs to tell him of the latest public relations crisis. Samuel had chosen to act on it immediately. His voice over the PA system promised, "We will have answers for you very soon. You make our task more difficult by being here. If you go home, we can finish our work that much more quickly."

It worked. People were used to listening to Samuel Grant II. And obeying. Once the crowd had gone, muttering among themselves, a huge sigh of relief seemed to sweep the ER.

"You can all go home now, too," Astrid Thompson told the volunteers. "You were here all day. Not a good idea to become overtired just now, right? And the crisis has passed for now, although that crowd will be back if your father doesn't deliver on his promise, Susannah."

Tired and upset about the new cases of fever, Susannah, Will, and Abby headed for the exit. Kate had announced that she was going upstairs to see how Damon was, maybe sit with him awhile.

"They won't let you in," Will told her.

"Yeah," she said with a grin, "they will."

Susannah regretted not having had more time to talk with Will. But even if he had asked to take her home, which he hadn't, she had her own car. He seemed more distant now than he had at the club, and she wondered if she'd made a mistake, asking him to dance. Maybe he was regretting having accepted.

She was too tired to think about that now. Maybe next week when, if her father delivered on his promise, they had some answers. She'd think about Will then. Right now, the fever was taking up so much space, there wasn't room for Will.

Susannah stayed at Abby's. No point in going home to argue with her mother. After the three new cases, Caroline couldn't possibly have changed her mind. Before she visited her brother, Susannah checked at the ICU reception desk to make sure her parents weren't in Sam's room.

The protests died down, as people awaited word from the CDC, as promised by Samuel Grant. The streets of the city remained deserted, and all Med Center or University social events scheduled for the week were canceled.

Driving to Abby's from the hospital on Monday evening, after one of the worst weekends she had ever endured, Susannah thought that it was as if the city of Grant, Massachusetts, had been evacuated. Yet all of the people were still there. They were hiding inside their homes, hoping the fever wouldn't find them there.

Zack called to tell her he and all the band members had been tested. "Haven't heard yet whether we passed or not," he said lightly, but she heard anxiety in his voice. She couldn't blame him. I'd be nervous, too, she thought. Who would want to be responsible for this awful disease?

Everyone was tense, waiting for answers from the CDC investigators, who were working around the clock at the Grant Pharmaceutical's massive lab.

At work, Will remained cool. Confused, Susannah avoided him. She was sure he regretted dancing with her. There were times when she wished she had never asked him, and vowed never to make the same mistake again. Other times, she blamed his attitude on the tension at

Emsee. No one was acting normally. Why should Will be the exception?

Late on Monday night, Susannah answered the telephone in Abby's room while Abby was taking a shower, and heard her father's voice.

"Susannah." His voice was low, urgent. "Your brother has taken a turn for the worse. Your mother needs you. You'll come right away." It wasn't a question.

"I'll be right there," she said, and hung up the phone.

chapter
24

Although the day had been clear, with a beautiful, cloudless blue sky, it was beginning to rain as Susannah, with Abby in the front seat beside her, sped to Med Center.

"If your mom is still mad at you, you'll need a friend there," Abby had insisted. Susannah hadn't argued. Even if her mother wasn't mad at her, she'd still need a friend at Emsee if Sam was . . . if Sam was . . . her mind refused to finish the thought.

By the time they ran from the parking garage, the rain was coming down steadily, pelting the ground and slapping against windows and roofs all over the complex.

Many of Sam's friends had gathered in the ER waiting room. They jumped to their feet when Susannah came rushing in. She had to tell them she knew nothing, that she hadn't even seen Sam yet. "How did you find out he was worse?" she asked Tom Cooper, one of Sam's soccer teammates.

"Callie called me. She's here, somewhere. Upstairs with her mother, I guess. She knows I call the hospital every night to see how Sam is, since we're not allowed in to see him. I was just about to call when the phone rang. Callie was really upset. She said there were all kinds of doctors and nurses rushing into Sam's room and that your parents looked really scared. So I called everyone together and we came over here. Don't you know anything?" he finished in a pleading voice.

"No. I'm sorry. I'll go up, and then I'll come back down and tell you, okay? If they tell me anything."

What she found out when she went upstairs was that Sam had stopped breathing. He had been resuscitated, but was now on life supports, like Damon. When Susannah looked in through the door window and saw her twin hooked up to even more machinery, her own heart nearly stopped. "Oh, God," she breathed to Abby, "he doesn't even look alive!"

"But he is, Susannah. He still is. You hold on to that."

Everything that could be done had been, Susannah was told. If Sam's vital organs didn't fail, they could "maintain" him, a word that made Susannah flinch, until a vaccine was made available, if that happened very quickly.

It didn't happen for the next two days. All the Grant family could do was wait. The only time they left the complex was for a quick shower and change of clothes. The rest of the time, they sat in the ICU waiting room, and what they did there was wait.

They weren't alone. Caleb and Callie Matthews were there, as well as relatives of the other patients who had family.

Kate took turns visiting Jenkins Rue and Damon Lawerence. The nurses in ICU no longer questioned her visits, since no one else ever showed up and asked to see the two.

On Thursday, the two CDC investigators, accompanied by Dr. Beck, called a meeting in Caleb Matthews's office. Susannah was allowed to attend.

"We know it isn't any of the musicians who played at the club," Dr. Cicero said when they were all seated. Caleb Matthews, looking physically drained, sat at his desk, clearly impatient for an answer that would save his wife. "They've all tested negative. And although they were ill on their last trip out of the country, we're fairly certain that was simply a reaction to the change in environment. One band member may have had a touch of the flu when they played in South America, but that's it."

Dr. Cicero repeatedly consulted her yellow-pad notes as she spoke. "With our computers and the help of our Atlanta staff, we've contacted every resident in the area who has traveled internationally within the past month. There weren't that many. By early this afternoon, we were able to narrow the possibilities down to only the four band members and one other person. Now that we've eliminated the band, that leaves only one more possibility." Dr. Cicero raised her eyes from the notepad in her lap. She looked at Samuel Grant. "I'm sorry, Mr. Grant. I know you were hoping otherwise, but we believe the person we're seeking may be your employee, Mr. Montgomery. The dead girl's father. We must get in touch with him immediately."

Susannah and Abby exchanged a horrified glance. Tina's father might be told that he had, however innocently, brought back from his South American trip an illness that had taken the life of his only child?

"What we've learned from his coworkers," Dr. Link interjected, "is, while Mr. Montgomery himself stayed pretty close to his city hotel, the people who came to him, bringing the new herb he was after, were indeed from a remote village, the place called Esperanza, deep in the rain forest, just as you told us, Mr. Grant. They came by boat. We believe this is a virus that is transmitted through animal or insect bite. One of the bearers could have been bitten on the trip by a mosquito, or perhaps a river rat. Or he might have been bitten by a monkey or bat before he began the trip. He couldn't have been symptomatic yet, or someone would have noticed. He wouldn't even have known that he was ill. I understand that two of the bearers failed to return to the village, that they quit their positions and disappeared. They may have returned to their own villages, and are probably dead. We've had no reports of any outbreaks similar to this one elsewhere, but we probably will, sooner or later. News doesn't travel as quickly in other parts of the world as it does here."

"And I was right," Dr. Beck added. "It is a new virus. For now, the CDC is simply calling it 'Esperanza fever.' They have begun a file and will add to it as new information comes in."

"Then," Samuel said heavily, "there is no cure. No vaccine."

"Not yet," Dr. Link said. "That's why we need Montgomery. He brought it back here. He had it. It just didn't affect him to any degree. You did say he had a touch of travel sickness?"

Samuel nodded.

"That probably was the fever. And he may have been sicker than he was willing to admit. The man has a strong immune system, I'll say that. At any rate, if we're right, if he did have it and recovered quickly, we can use his antibodies to create a vaccine."

"How long will that take?" Samuel's eyes were anxious.

"Not long. Your lab is beautifully set up for

what we need to do. In the meantime, if any of the current patients worsen, we'll put them on life supports until the vaccine is ready, and do everything we can to protect their vital organs from serious damage."

"Montgomery isn't here," Samuel said. "I told you, he's in the Berkshires, at our lodge. There is no telephone."

"Someone will have to take one of us up there to get him," Dr. Cicero said matter-of-factly. "Now."

Susannah stood up. "I'll go."

"No!" Caroline stood up, too. "Not you." Her eyes were not cold with anger. They were warm and pleading. "Please, Susannah, I need you here. Someone else can go."

"Mother, I know how to get to the lodge."

"I'll hire a driver," Samuel said.

"No, I'll go," Abby volunteered. "I've been there. I remember where it is. We shouldn't waste time hiring someone."

Susannah hesitated. She wanted Abby with her. But she could see that Abby was determined to be helpful. "Take the Benz. It'd take too long to go home and get your station wagon. Besides, those roads curve like snakes, and the Benz can turn on a dime."

Abby nodded. "Thanks."

"I'll go with you," Dr. Link volunteered. "Cicero and Beck have work to do here, at the lab."

Susannah was torn. It was raining again, had been since late that afternoon. She didn't really want Abby driving all the way up to the Berkshires on such a nasty night. But Sam was just barely hanging on. Time was crucial. They couldn't afford to wait until tomorrow for someone to fetch Mr. Montgomery.

She let out a deep breath. "Okay, Abby. We owe you."

"Don't mention it. C'mon, Dr. Link," Abby said cheerfully, "let's go bring the man back alive. Keys, Sooz?"

Susannah handed her the keys.

But when they'd gone, she had to fight an impulse to run after Abby and the young doctor. Telling herself that she was probably just upset about Sam's worsening condition, and telling herself that if anyone she knew could take care of herself, it was Abby, Susannah turned to join her parents in Sam's room.

Abby wasn't willing to admit aloud to Dr. Link that although the Benz *was* handling like a dream in spite of the slick roads, she was having trouble seeing the road that snaked up the hill, flanked by thick, dark woods on both sides. If she'd remembered correctly, they'd be at the lodge in four or five minutes. Why give the doctor something new to worry about?

It was almost dawn, although since the rain hadn't lessened at all, there was no sign of a rising sun off to the east. The horizon was heavy only with dark, gray clouds. They'd be driving back in pouring rain, too.

The Montgomerys would be asleep. There hadn't been any way to warn them that someone was coming to drag them out of bed and give them more bad news. Horrible news.

"You have to tell them," she said as the lodge appeared in view at the top of a hill ahead of them. "I got us here. You be the bearer of bad tidings, okay? I can't do it."

"I'm not planning on telling them that

much," Dr. Link said. "Only that Mr. Montgomery is needed back at Med Center. He won't be surprised. He knows there's a crisis there."

"His daughter died last week," Abby said soberly as she pulled up the long, narrow driveway curving up the hill. "Won't he think it's pretty callous of us to be dragging him back to work?"

"It *is* pretty callous. But absolutely necessary. And remember, this man, if Cicero is right, will be saving many lives. I don't think he'll give us a hard time."

He didn't. Although he and his wife were clearly upset at being disturbed, Montgomery was used to being called to duty at odd times, on an emergency basis. Abby even had a feeling as they all left the house and the Montgomerys climbed into their Cadillac, that, in a way, the man was relieved to be going back to work.

She felt bad for him. Any other time, work might have been the best cure for his grief. If Dr. Cicero weren't awaiting him at Med Center with some awful news.

"Poor guy," Dr. Link said as Abby, in the lead car, carefully steered the Benz back down the steep hill. "I wouldn't want to be in his shoes."

"Well," she said as they arrived on the main road, "maybe Dr. Cicero will think to tell Tina's father what you said before, that he'll be saving lives. It won't bring Tina back, but it's still a good thing. And it wasn't his fault that she got sick, right?"

"No. Definitely not his fault. There are going to be more of these fevers hitting the populace from time to time," Dr. Link told her, "as people dig deeper into unknown territory. And there's the other side of the coin, too, which is that every time we plunge into these remote areas, we bring disease with *us*, threatening the lives of the natives already living there. So we're not the only victims, just in case you thought we were."

"Until this disgusting fever came along," Abby replied, peering into the thick sheet of rain pelting the car, "I hadn't thought about it at all, Dr. Link. But I will now. I promise you that."

By the time they were on the outskirts of Grant, she was exhausted. Every bone and muscle in her body ached. Her eyes felt gritty. Her head ached. But she had stayed awake! All night long. Something to be proud of. She'd done something good. Maybe not for Mr. Montgomery, who was about to get his second major shock in two weeks. But for the others in ICU. Like Sam.

She could only hope they were in time.

She glanced in the rearview mirror. The Montgomerys were still right behind them, the Caddy hugging the road every bit as snugly as the Benz.

Her eyes went back to the road only a fraction of a second too late. Weather conditions being what they were, even a moment's distraction was too much. The right side of the car swerved off the road and onto the rain-soaked soft shoulder. Too late, Abby realized her mistake. Gasping, she struggled with the steering wheel, whipping it to the left to force the car back on track. But the right wheels had sunk into the wet, muddy berm and refused to leave it. She slammed on the brake, her second mistake. The small, silver car spun around in a semicircle, then left the road completely, slamming into the guardrail now on Abby's side, where it shouldn't have been. The guardrail gave, and the car, totally out of control, flew through the broken rail and careened down the slippery, sodden hill, gathering speed as it went.

When Abby saw the huge, gnarled old tree, thick and forbidding, looming up out of the rain suddenly at midpoint on the hill, she knew they were going to hit it. Her hands frozen to the steering wheel, she tried with all her strength to wrest it left or right, didn't matter which, any direction at all if it meant missing that enormous tree. But the car refused to obey any of her commands and it was going faster and faster, though she'd long since taken her shaking foot off the accelerator.

There was no way they could miss that tree, which looked like a stone barricade in the middle of the hill. And might as well have been.

"Get down!" Dr. Link shouted frantically, and an arm shot out to shove Abby's head down into her lap.

Her last thought before they hit was, Now we're not going to get there in time to help Sam.

She would have screamed in terror then. If there had been time. But there wasn't.

chapter
26

On Friday morning, Will was on the ambulance dispatched to a rainy slope on the outskirts of Grant.

"Oh, my God," he whispered as he helped pull an injured girl from the crumpled heap of silver metal lying at the base of an enormous tree. In spite of the blood streaking her face and hair, in spite of the thick cervical collar already applied to her neck inside the car before she was gently placed on the backboard, Will knew her instantly. "It's Abby! Oh, man, how can I tell Susannah about this? First Sam, now Abby?"

Abby opened her eyes. "Oh, relax, Will, I'll tell her myself," she said weakly. Will's knees went limp with relief as he laughed aloud. "Don't ever scare me like that again!"

"Okay, I won't. I promise."

Will and his partner carried Abby to the ambulance. She had a deep laceration on her forehead, a shallow but wider one on her chin, and a third, the most serious, on her right shoulder. But miraculously, she seemed to have no other injuries and her vital signs indicated no internal injuries. Will couldn't believe it. Susannah's car looked like it had been processed through a compactor. "You're going to be fine, Abby. Just lie still, okay? But," Will said, smiling, "you're a real mess. Can't you do something with your hair?"

She smiled back. "Nope, never could. How's Dr. Link?"

The doctor hadn't fared as well as Abby. "My chest . . ." he had gasped as they gently placed him on a stretcher. "Hurts . . ." When Will checked, his abdomen was tender, his breathing was labored, and the young doctor was fading from consciousness quickly.

"Pulse 140, respirations 36 and shallow, BP 70/50," Will's partner said. "Breath sounds diminished on right side. I think we'd better phone in, fast. Let's get him inside."

In the ambulance, they obeyed the orders from the hospital, setting up the IVs and, when the rapid infusion of fluids failed to affect the blood pressure, applying antishock trousers and inflating them.

"What's wrong with him?" Abby asked from her gurney.

"I don't know for sure," Will told her. "Chest injury, maybe something internal, too."

"He's not going to die, is he? I think he saved my life. Made me put my head down right before we hit."

"He won't die," Will said confidently. "But he'll be on his way to surgery as soon as they put a chest tube into him in ER and take X rays to see what's going on inside."

"Good." Abby closed her eyes.

Susannah had just come downstairs to get coffee for everyone in the ICU waiting room when the ambulance pulled up outside. She automatically turned around, one hand still on the coffeepot's faucet, watching the doors to see how bad the damage was as the gurney came racing by.

She would have known that dark curly hair anywhere, even rain-soaked and streaked with blood. And she knew, she knew with sickening certainty, why she hadn't felt right about letting her best friend drive all the way up to the Berkshires on such an awful night. Because she'd known something terrible would happen. And it had.

"Abby?" Susannah asked hoarsely. "Abby?" The Styrofoam cup filled with hot coffee dropped from her hand and landed on the white tile with a plopping sound and a thick spray of dark brown. The hallway began spinning crazily. She saw Will's dark eyes glancing over at her as he passed, she saw the blood on Abby's cheek, forehead, and chin. Her stomach mimicked the hallway's crazy spinning.

She would have fallen then if she hadn't heard

Astrid Thompson's voice saying inside her dizzily spinning mind, "Being allowed in the treatment rooms without any formal medical training is an honor, Susannah. It's being given you because the consensus is that you can handle it. It will be rough at times, sometimes very rough. But we believe you're strong enough."

She couldn't pass out. She was exhausted from the strain of the past weeks and would have liked nothing more at that moment than to slide to the floor and wait for someone to pick her up, put her on a gurney, and take her away to a peaceful, quiet, treatment room to sleep for days.

But Abby needed her.

Susannah jerked upright, stiffening her spine. And noticed instantly that Abby's eyes were open . . . they were open! . . . she was *alive* . . . she hadn't died.

Abby's mouth opened as well, and although she was shaking with cold and shock, which made her voice unsteady, it was clear enough. "You look like you're staring at a ghost, Susannah. Stop that. I might think I actually *am* one."

Susannah managed a weak laugh. "Well, you're not. You are very much alive. Now shut up and let the doctors be nice to you."

While Abby's lacerations, only one of which required stitches, were being tended to, Dr. Link was sent upstairs to surgery for a lacerated liver. Susannah was assured he would be fine.

"We're going to keep Abby here overnight," Susannah was told when Abby had been treated. "I'm sure she's fine, but she took quite a ride down that hill according to Will, and we'd like to keep an eye on her. You can go up and see her when she's settled."

On her way back to Sam's room, Susannah saw Mr. Montgomery emerging from an office in the company of Dr. Cicero. He was wiping tears from his face with a white handkerchief. Susannah's heart ached for him.

But in the next minute, she saw him straighten his shoulders, take a deep breath, and let it out. Then he headed in the direction of the lab with the doctor for the blood tests. He looked like a man with a purpose.

Susannah had no idea why Mr. Montgomery hadn't been ravaged by the fever. He was strong and healthy, but so were her brother Sam and Jenkins Rue. It was rare, but Montgomery must have had an inborn immunity to the disease. He hadn't even known he had it. Now the antibodies in his blood would save others from getting it.

He's going to save them, she thought with certainty. He's going to save all of them. The ones who have the fever now, and the others who might have had it if it weren't for Tina Montgomery's father. Dr. Cicero and the other doctors will use his antibodies to create a vaccine. They'll do it quickly, thanks to my father's lab, and after a while, ICU will no longer be under quarantine. Sam and his friend will be out playing soccer and baseball and dating every girl in town. Jenkins Rue will be fishing off the riverbank. That girl will be back on Rollerblades, and Damon Lawrence will be racing around town in that old truck of his. The other people up in ICU will be back home where they belong, back at work or school, back to normal. I will have my brother back, and Callie will have her mother back.

But no one in this town, Susannah told herself with conviction, will ever forget that this happened.

It wasn't over yet, she knew that. They would have to keep all of the victims alive until the vaccine was ready. That would take every bit of medical knowledge available. It would take diligence, vigilance, and a whole lot of caring.

But then, there wasn't any place in the world with more of those things than Med Center.

Callie, upstairs visiting her mother, heard about the accident and came downstairs to find out how Abby was. She had just rounded the corner into the ER waiting room when Jeremy came in through the front door. "My father's going to go to breakfast with me," he told Callie with determination, "or I'm going to California to live with my mother. That's the deal. He can take it or leave it. No more sitting on the sidelines, waiting for him."

He expected Callie to say, "Good for you, Jeremy!" Instead, she said, "I thought you were here because you heard about Abby's accident."

Jeremy's face paled. "Abby? What accident?"

When Susannah had explained to them that Abby was in no serious danger, she was quick to add the news about Mr. Montgomery.

Callie's face flooded with relief. "Oh, God, I've got to go tell my mother! Oh, Susannah, thank you, thanks for telling me!" She whirled and ran.

"Does Kate know?" Jeremy asked Susannah.

"Does Kate know what?" Kate asked as she came up behind them. She tossed her shoulder bag into a cupboard, and grabbed her smock off a peg and slipped it on over a pink-and-purple tie-dyed T-shirt. "What's happening that I don't know about?"

Susannah explained about the accident, and added the news about Mr. Montgomery. "So," she finished with a smile, "looks like you're going to have to model in my mother's fashion show, after all, Kate. It's not going to be canceled."

Kate ran a pick through her bangs, then slipped the pick into her jeans pocket. "Well, at least Abby's okay," she said. "We all owe her for driving all the way up there to bring Montgomery back, right?"

Susannah and Jeremy nodded.

"And," Kate added with a grin, "it just so happens I *like* the idea of modeling. Maybe an editor from a fashion magazine will spot me up there on that runway and offer me big bucks to grace her cover. I'll become as world-famous as Med Center, make zillions of dollars, date rock stars and professional football players, and you can all say you knew me when."

Jeremy looked at her with concern, but Susannah laughed. "Relax, Jeremy! She'd last about two seconds in the modeling business. People telling her where to sit, where to stand, how to smile? I think half the reason Kate is going to become a doctor is so she can tell people what to do. I can't see her sitting on some beach in February, freezing to death in a bikini."

Jeremy did relax. He grinned. "I can see her in a bikini."

"Quit leering," Kate said with mock disapproval. "If you're on your way upstairs, I'll go with you. I want to see how Damon is. If he's awake, I'll give him the good news about Montgomery."

"You going up to see Sam?" Will's voice asked suddenly from over Susannah's shoulder.

She turned around. "Yes. Want to come? You can't go in to see him. But . . ." she hesitated, wondering if this was the right time. Maybe not. He had pulled away from her again after that one dance at The Music Room.

But the past two weeks had taught her that maybe it wasn't such a hot idea to wait for "the right time." Something could come along and knock "the right time" right off the clock.

Deciding, Susannah said, "I'm on my way up to tell my parents that Abby brought Mr. Montgomery back, and that a vaccine is on the way. You could come up and say hello to them."

Susannah almost smiled then at the look of uncertainty that spread across Will's face. Will, who was always so confident. "I've never even met them," he said.

"I know." She did smile then. "I'm asking you if you want to. Now."

It was his turn to hesitate.

It doesn't mean a commitment, Susannah wanted to say. Meeting my parents doesn't mean I'm asking you for anything. It just means that I want you to meet them. And that you're ready to. That's all it means.

Although she didn't say any of that aloud, he might have seen it in her eyes, because he said then, "Yeah. Sure. I guess I can say hello to them. Anyway," he added quickly, "I wanted to see how Damon and Jenkins are doing. I'll check that out while I'm up there."

"Right," Susannah said, still smiling as she pushed the elevator button.

While they waited for the cage to arrive, she glanced around ER, at the staff moving quickly from room to room, the orderlies pushing gurneys or wheelchairs along the hallway, other volunteers her age in pink smocks marching along armed with magazines and hospital menus. When school began again in September, she would have to cut back on her volunteer time. They all would. But for now, she thought with satisfaction, this is where I want to be.

Then, as the elevator doors began to slide closed upon her and Will, she caught a glimpse of a white-faced young man, a red-stained, pale yellow towel wrapped around his left hand, as he rushed in through the doorway, calling, "I need help here!"

As two nurses and a resident ran to his aid, Susannah sent a mental message to the injured boy. You have come to the right place, she told him silently. Just. Like. Me.

The elevator doors slid shut.

An exciting excerpt from *Flood*, Med Center #2, coming next.

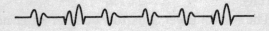

It began raining in Grant, Massachusetts, at 11:23 on a Tuesday night in mid-September. It rained lightly at first, a pleasant, refreshing, early autumn shower. Gardeners all over the city welcomed it, after ten straight days with no moisture for their fall gardens and the last of their roses.

During that night and most of the next day, the parched ground eagerly soaked up the falling rain.

But by the following evening, as commuters were making their way home, the pleasant shower turned nasty, throwing a temper tantrum. The wind rose, tearing at limbs of the huge old trees lining both sides of Linden Hill Boulevard, the main artery between the east and west sides of town. The skies turned an ominous black and, seconds later, opened, dumping thick torrents of rain, flooding streets with deep washes of water, and snarling traffic throughout the city. The already saturated ground refused to accept this additional drink of water and spilled it out into the streets. Stubborn drivers intent on making it home drove through rushing pockets of water at low-lying intersections, a mistake that resulted in wet, ineffective brakes, which in turn caused a series of "fender-bender" accidents throughout the city.

The Revere River, a narrow body of water normally ambling its way peacefully through Grant, began to swell, edging up the riverbanks on both sides like water filling a bathtub.

On the west side of the river, nestled on a knoll in the heart of the city, the world-famous medical complex known as Med Center stood staunchly against the onslaught of rain and wind. At Grant Memorial Hospital, the tallest of eighteen red brick buildings in varying shapes and sizes, Astrid Thompson, head nurse in Emergency Services, peered out a rain-streaked window and exclaimed, "Oh, great! A storm during rush hour. Just what we need. Step lively, everyone, it's going to be an interesting night!"

It was.